Second Edition

Grammar Troublespots

An Editing Guide for Students

ANN RAIMES

Hunter College,
The City University of New York

CAMBRIDGE UNIVERSITY PRESS

PUBLISHED BY THE PRESS SYNDICATE OF THE UNIVERSITY OF CAMBRIDGE
The Pitt Building, Trumpington Street, Cambridge, United Kingdom

CAMBRIDGE UNIVERSITY PRESS
The Edinburgh Building, Cambridge CB2 2RU, UK
40 West 20th Street, New York, NY 10011–4211, USA
477 Williamstown Road, Port Melbourne, VIC 3207, Australia
Ruiz de Alarcón 13, 28014 Madrid, Spain
Dock House, The Waterfront, Cape Town 8001, South Africa

http://www.cambridge.org

First published by St. Martin's Press, Inc. 1992

5th printing 2003

Printed in the United States of America

Library of Congress Cataloging-in-Publication Data Available

ISBN 0 521 65759 8 Student's Book

Acknowledgment
page 142: *Peanuts* cartoon. Copyright © 1959. Reprinted by U.F.S., Inc.

Preface: To the Instructor

Grammar Troublespots: An Editing Guide for Students, second edition, offers a modified version of the grammar editing section that is included in *Exploring Through Writing: A Process Approach to ESL Composition*, second edition (St. Martin's Press, 1992). There it is part of a whole course built around reading, pictures, and guided instruction through the writing process. Here it is designed either to be used independently by students as they edit their college writing assignments or to accompany whatever course material a writing instructor selects. This book then functions as an editing guide, presenting ways of looking at and critically examining any piece of writing in order to edit it for standard grammar and syntax.

In a writing course, it is recommended that students work through a few sections in class, perhaps *Troublespots 1, 5,* and *11,* either as a whole-class or group activity, each time using authentic pieces of student writing from that class to examine and edit. In this way, as teachers and students ask questions about the sentences on the page in front of them, students see models for the process of examining their own work and applying grammatical principles. Grammatical vocabulary is introduced for editing purposes but is kept simple; for example, *subject, predicate, noun, verb, article, clause, singular,* and *plural* are clear, key concepts for editing purposes. Once students have used several flowcharts and have become familiar with the limited grammatical terminology used in the book, they are able to use the rest of the book independently or as they are referred to specific chapters by their instructor.

The Second Edition

In response to instructors' feedback, the following changes have been made:

Information on questions, negatives, commas, and apostrophes has been included in other troublespots, while new sections have been added to pay more attention to punctuation, verb tenses, modal auxiliaries, infinitives, and prepositions.

Explanations and exercises are differentiated and numbered separately in each troublespot.

More exercises have been included.

Also in response to instructors' requests, the structure of the book—the many illustrative charts and boxes, and the flowcharts that constantly send students back to examine their own writing in concrete and specific ways—has been retained.

Ann Raimes

Contents

Introduction

Grammar Troublespots, second edition, offers you help with some important "grammar troublespots" of English that might cause you difficulties in your writing. It is not intended to be a complete review of English grammar, nor is it intended to cover everything you need to know to correct all errors in a piece of writing. Rather, the book concentrates on rules, not exceptions, so it will help you apply general principles. It will also aid you in finding ways to examine and evaluate your own writing in terms of grammatical accuracy.

In *Grammar Troublespots* you will discover explanations for some conventions of standard written English—areas of the language that operate systematically, according to rules. These explanations are accompanied by exercises (an *Answer Key* is included at the back of the book) and by flowcharts that give you specific questions to ask as you evaluate your own writing. By focusing your attention directly on the problem area, these questions will help you find and correct your own errors, either independently or with the help of an instructor. Sometimes, such focusing is precisely what a writer needs in order to find—and correct—errors.

The editing advice given frequently suggests that you seek help: from a classmate, from your instructor, or from a dictionary. Certainly a dictionary such as *Oxford Student's Dictionary of American English* (Oxford University Press, 1983) or *The American Heritage Dictionary of the English Language: New College Edition* (Houghton Mifflin, 1983) is an invaluable tool for checking not only spelling but also irregular plural forms, verb forms, and idioms. Experienced writers often seek advice, so make sure to use the resources around you.

Throughout this book, a sentence preceded by an asterisk (*) indicates an *example sentence* that is not acceptable in standard edited English.

TROUBLESPOT 1

Basic Sentence Structure

Exercise 1

The following lines appeared in students' essays describing vacation spots and beach scenes. Which ones are standard sentences in written English and which ones are not?

1. the sun is shining.
2. They walk slowly and quietly
3. Watching themselves make steps on the white sand.
4. You can hardly see any sand.
5. Because there are so many people and so many umbrellas.
6. You can imagine walking on the white glittering sand.
7. The feeling of cool sand running through your toes.
8. There is a big coconut tree.
9. Some leaves on the sand.
10. Is a St. Croix beach in the Virgin Islands.
11. The tree on the beach it is very big.
12. Shade from the sun some umbrellas provide.
13. On that beach, two people who are enjoying the beautiful weather.
14. The sun shining.
15. The people who are sitting on the beach feel very relaxed.

Write a correct version of each numbered line that is not a sentence. You can correct the grammar or punctuation, or combine one numbered line with the one that comes before or after it in the list. (See Answer Key, p. 152.) When you have finished, list what you consider the requirements of a sentence to be.

A. Subject and Predicate

In the following short sentence

Babies cry.

we find elements common to all sentences. The sentence has a topic: The *topic* is *babies*. Frequently, the topic of the sentence is the grammatical *subject* of the sentence. The sentence makes a *comment* about the topic: We learn that *babies* (our topic) *cry*. This comment forms the *predicate* of the sentence.

Some more examples follow:

Subject	*Predicate*
Babies	cry.
The babies next door	cry a lot.
Her baby	does not cry much.
My brother	likes ice cream.
Some big towels	are lying on the sand.
The tree on the beach	is very big.
Crowds	can spoil a vacation resort.
The two people walking on the beach	look very happy.
I	have never been to the Caribbean.

Note that a sentence other than a command must contain a subject and a predicate. The predicate must contain a complete verb, one that indicates time. For example:

She *has been working.*
They *will work.*
He *has worked.*

(See Troublespots 5 and 11 for further examples of verbs and verb tenses.)

Exercise 2

Divide the following sentences into subject and predicate.

1. We lived in Shin-Ying.
2. The front door of the house faced the front gate of the elementary school.
3. My mother taught at the school.

4. Cleaning up the fallen leaves was my job.
5. My family sat around under the grapevine.

(See Answer Key, p. 152.)

B. Avoiding Sentence Fragments

A sentence fragment is an incomplete sentence. It can occur when a subject is missing, when there is not a complete verb, or when there is no subject–predicate structure in an independent clause. Examples of fragments in Exercise 1 are items 3, 5, 7, 9, 10, 13, and 14.

Exercise 3

Some of the following student writing samples contain a group of words that is *not* a sentence, even though it has a capital letter and end punctuation. It is only part of a sentence (that is, a *sentence fragment*). Determine which groups of words are fragments. Then decide how you could turn the fragment into a complete sentence or include it in another sentence.

1. (a) The dark scenery could frighten us. (b) Because there are many trees.
2. (a) He is working at the gas pumps. (b) To try to fix what is wrong.
3. (a) The soft crashing waves and the shade cast by a tall palm tree make this an attractive spot. (b) One that we would really like to return to.
4. (a) People are lying on the beach and getting a suntan. (b) Because it is a holiday, the beach is packed.
5. (a) On that peaceful beach, two young people strolling along the water's edge. (b) They look happy.

(See Answer Key, p. 153.)

C. Requirements of a Written Sentence

Compare your list of the requirements of a sentence (in Exercise 1) to the requirements shown in the accompanying box. How many of these requirements did you write on your list?

REQUIREMENTS OF A WRITTEN SENTENCE

A capital letter at the beginning

A period, a question mark, or an exclamation point at the end

A subject, stated only once (*There* and *it* can act as filler subjects.)

A complete verb phrase—that is, any auxiliaries, such as *is, were, has, had, will, can, might, would, should, have, would have,* and *will be,* along with the verb forms used to form the verb phrase (See Troublespot 11, "Verb Forms.")

Standard word order: in English, the regular sequence is S + V + O (subject + verb + object), with insertions possible at several points in the sequence

An independent core idea that can stand alone (This is known as a *main clause* or, as we call it in this book, an *independent clause.*)

D. Word Order

Every language has its own conventions for word order. The normal word order in an English sentence is

S	V	O/C
subject	verb	object or complement (after linking verbs like *be, feel, look*)

Children	like	cookies.
She	eats	a lot of candy.
My old boss	has bought	a new car.
He	is	a teacher.
They	look	happy.

Do not separate verb and object: S V-O

He bought a new car yesterday.
OR   Yesterday he bought a new car.
NOT *He bought yesterday a new car.

Put time expressions (T) first or last in the sentence:

T, S V O
OR S V O T

Almost every day, she drinks five glasses of water.
OR   She drinks five glasses of water almost every day.
NOT *She drinks almost every day five glasses of water.

E. Direct and Indirect Objects

Note the word order for direct and indirect objects:

S	V	Direct O	to/for + Indirect O
She	gave	her tape recorder	to her aunt.

S	V	Indirect O	Direct O
She	gave	her aunt	her tape recorder.

When the indirect object is a pronoun, only the second alternative can be used:

S	V	Indirect O	Direct O
She	gave	me	a plant.

F. Inverted Word Order: V + S

The usual word order is S + V + O/C. However, the verb comes before the subject in instances like the following:

1. In direct questions

Do you like chocolate ice cream? *Have you* ever eaten lobster?

2. In coordinate tags

She likes swimming and so *do I.*

(See also Troublespots 2 and 11.)

3. For emphasis after *never* or *not only* at the beginning of a sentence:

Never have I seen such a lot of waste!
Never will that happen!
Not only did she arrive late, but she also forgot to bring some food.
Not only will he repair the computer, but he will also do it without charge.

4. When *if* is omitted

Had I the time, I would paint my room.

G. Parallel Structures

Structures that fill the same position in a sentence must be parallel in form. The word *and* connects similar structures:

NOT *They want to feel cool and happily.
BUT They want to feel cool and happy.

NOT *I want to go to Italy and spending a week in Venice.
BUT I want to go to Italy and spend a week in Venice.

H. Adding Information to an Independent Clause

Sentences can be long or short, simple or complex. This is a simple sentence:

The man bought a new car.

It contains one independent clause (a sentence that makes sense alone and can stand alone). This independent clause has a verb, *bought,* and a subject for the verb, the person who did the buying, *the man.* In addition, it has an object, telling us what the man bought—*a new car.* However, we can add other information, too, and the sentence will still have only one independent clause. It will just be a longer sentence. We can add information at several points within the sentence, and that information can take the form of different grammatical structures:

1. *Add information at the beginning.*

Last week, the man bought a new car.
Because he felt adventurous, the man bought a new car.
Although his wife hated the idea, the man bought a new car.
Wanting to impress his friends, the man bought a new car.
Bored with his life in the city, the man bought a new car.
To try to impress his friends, the man bought a new car.

2. *Expand the subject.*

The rich man bought a new car.
The man who got a raise last week bought a new car.
The man who works in my office bought a new car.
The man working in my office bought a new car.
The man and his wife bought a new car.
The man with the old Cadillac bought a new car.

3. Insert some additional information in the middle.

The man in my office, Joseph Moran, bought a new car.
The man, wanting to impress his friends, bought a new car.
The man, proud and excited about his raise in salary, bought a new car.

4. Expand the verb.

The man bought and sold a new car.
The man bought a new car and sold it.

5. Expand the object.

The man bought a fancy new red car.
The man bought a new car and a computer.
The man bought his wife a new car. (indirect object/direct object)
The man bought a new car for his wife. (direct object/indirect object with
to or *for*)

6. Add information at the end.

The man bought a new car last week.
The man bought a new car because he felt adventurous.
The man bought a new car when he could afford it.
The man bought a new car to try to impress his friends.
The man bought a new car even though his wife didn't approve.

Note that in each of the preceding sentences, there is only one clause (a subject + verb combination) that can stand alone—the independent clause.

Exercise 4

Expand the following sentence by adding information in different places. See how many variations you can invent. Refer to item H for examples of structures that you might add.

The doctor prescribed some pills.

Exercise 5

Now you can test yourself to see how well you can identify standard sentences in written English. The following sentences were written by students.

Which are standard sentences in written English and which are not? Make any corrections necessary.

1. Dogs bark.
2. (a) The children in the park are eating some delicious ice cream cones. (b) Because they want to get cool.
3. They eating very slowly.
4. The children who were eating the ice cream they were with my uncle.
5. Usually in the summer is very hot in the city.
6. She spends every week a lot of money.
7. He likes very much his sister's friend.
8. She gave to her sister an expensive present.
9. On a beach, nature gives you tranquillity and peace without noisy, pollution, crowded, dirt, and humid.
10. The smell of frying hot dogs filling my nostrils and making me hungry.

(See Answer Key, p. 153.)

Editing Advice

Use the following flowchart with a piece of your writing to examine any sentences that you think might have a problem in structure. Begin with the last sentence of your draft and work backward. In this way, you can isolate each sentence from its context and examine it more objectively. Ask these questions for each problematic sentence:

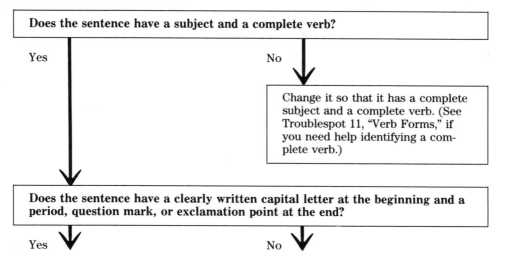

Does the sentence have a subject and a complete verb?

Yes   No

Change it so that it has a complete subject and a complete verb. (See Troublespot 11, "Verb Forms," if you need help identifying a complete verb.)

Does the sentence have a clearly written capital letter at the beginning and a period, question mark, or exclamation point at the end?

Yes   No

(Flowchart continued)

Yes

No

Add one.

Does the sentence include an independent clause (a core idea that can stand alone)?

Yes

No

If the only clause (subject and verb combination) is introduced with a word such as *when*, *if*, or *because*, either remove that word or attach the whole group of words to another independent clause. (If you need help, turn to Troublespot 3, "Combining Sentences with Subordinating Conjunctions."

Check to see that everything else is correctly connected to that independent clause. Check for word order, inversions, and parallel structures.

TROUBLESPOT 2

Connecting Sentences with Coordinating Conjunctions and Transitions

A. *Ways to Connect Sentences*

There are several ways to connect sentences to form a coordinate sentence that contains two or more core ideas (that is, independent clauses of equal importance). Which way you choose will depend on what best fits the content and context of your piece of writing. So consider all the options, in context, before you decide. The options are explained here.

1. When sentences are closely connected and their structure is similar, connect them by using a semicolon:

$$S \; + \; V; \qquad S \; + \; V.$$

The man bought a new car; his son borrowed it immediately.
My mother took care of the housework; my father earned the money.

2. You can also indicate how two independent clauses are related in meaning within a sentence if you coordinate the two clauses by using a comma followed by one of the following connecting words or *coordinating conjunctions:*

	and	
	but	
	so	
	or	
independent clause,	nor	independent clause.
S + V ,	for	S + V .
	yet	

The man bought a new car, *but* his wife didn't know about it.
He bought the gas, *and* his son paid for the repairs.

> Note that the structures on either side of the conjunction are parallel in form.

3. Two independent clauses with the same subject can also be condensed into one sentence:

The man bought a new car.
The man sold his old one.
The man bought a new car and sold his old one.

> No comma separates the two verbs when they have the same subject.

B. Transitions

There are also many linking expressions, called *transitions*, that help point out how sentences are joined according to meaning. Even if you use one of these expressions, you still need to separate your sentences with a period or a semicolon at the end of the first independent clause.

$$S \ + \ V \ ; \text{(transition)}, S \ + \ V \ .$$

The little girl had always hated spiders. *In fact*, she was terrified of them.
The little girl had always hated spiders; *in fact*, she was terrified of them.

TRANSITIONS

Writer's purpose	Transitional words and phrases
To add an idea	in addition, furthermore, moreover, also
To show time or sequence	meanwhile, first, second, then, next, later, finally
To contrast	however, nevertheless, though, in contrast, on the other hand
To show result	therefore, thus, consequently, as a result
To emphasize	in fact, of course, indeed, certainly
To provide an example	for example, for instance
To generalize or summarize	in general, overall, in short
To contradict	on the contrary

Transitions can also move around in the sentence:

The little girl had always hated spiders. She was, *in fact*, terrified of them.
The little girl had always hated spiders. She was terrified of them, *in fact.*

Transitions are set off from the rest of the sentence by commas. Some of the most frequently used transitional expressions are shown in the accompanying box. The expressions are not necessarily interchangeable. The context determines which is appropriate. If you want to use a transition but are not sure which one to use, ask your instructor.

Exercise 1

The following passages are from an article called "The Changing Family in International Perspective." Examine the use of transitions throughout the passages. List them and write the author's purpose in employing them. What kind of meaning do they signal between two ideas? Use the "Transitions" box to help you.

1. Household composition patterns over the past several decades have been away from the traditional nuclear family . . . and toward more single-parent households, more persons living alone, and more couples living together out of wedlock. Indeed, the "consensual union" has become a more visible and accepted family type in several countries.
2. Scandinavian countries have been the pacesetters in the development of many of the nontraditional forms of family living, especially births outside of wedlock and cohabitation outside of legal marriage. Women in these societies also have the highest rates of labor force participation. However, in at least two aspects, the United States is setting the pace.
3. Japan is the most traditional society of those studied, with very low rates of divorce and births out of wedlock and the highest proportion of married-couple households. In fact, Japan is the only country studied in which the share of such households has increased since 1960.
4. A trend toward fewer marriages is plain in all of the countries studied, although the timing of this decline differs from country to country. In Scandinavia and Germany, for example, the downward trend in the marriage rate was already evident in the 1960's.
5. Divorce laws were loosened in most European countries beginning in the 1970's, with further liberalization taking place in the 1980's. Consequently, divorce rates are rising rapidly in many European countries.

(See Answer Key, p. 152.)

Exercise 2

Connect the following pairs of sentences by using punctuation only, coordinating conjunctions, or transitions. You need to determine the relationship between the two sentences before you can choose a conjunction or a transition. Write as many new combined sentences as you can.

1. Hemingway had some peculiarities as a writer.
   He always wrote standing up.
2. Hemingway was a gifted journalist, novelist, and short-story writer.
   He was an active sportsman.
3. Hemingway did most of his writing in pencil on onionskin typewriter paper.
   He shifted to his typewriter when the writing was easy for him, as when writing dialogue.
4. Hemingway's room looked untidy at first glance.
   He was a neat person at heart.
5. Hemingway was a sentimental man, keeping his possessions all around him.
   He hardly ever threw anything away.
6. Hemingway always did a surprising amount of rewriting of his novels.
   He rewrote the ending of *A Farewell to Arms* 39 times.
7. Hemingway wrote his short story "The Killers" in one morning.
   After lunch, he wrote "Today Is Friday" and "Ten Indians."
8. Hemingway often wrote all through the afternoon and evening without stopping.
   His landlady worried that he wasn't eating enough.

(See Answer Key, p. 153.)

Exercise 3

Connect or combine the following pairs of sentences in two different ways, using first a coordinating conjunction and then a transition.

Example:

He wanted to have his name on a building.
He left money to build a new library.
He wanted to have his name on a building, so he left money to build a new library.
He wanted to have his name on a building; therefore, he left money to build a new library.

1. He injured his knee.
   He decided not to cancel his tennis game.
2. They visited France, Italy, and Spain.
   They managed to include Malta, Sardinia, and Majorca in their trip.
3. Their money was stolen.
   They got it all back because it was in traveler's checks.
4. She wanted to pass her exams.
   She studied every night in the semester.
5. She studied very hard.
   She didn't pass her examinations.

(See Answer Key, p. 154.)

C. Avoiding the Run-on Sentence and the Comma Splice

You cannot just follow one independent clause with another, with no punctuation:

NOT *The man bought a new car his wife didn't know about it.

This is a run-on sentence. Here you need a period or a semicolon after the word *car*.

And not even a comma by itself is enough to connect two independent clauses:

NOT *The man bought a new car, his wife didn't know about it.

This is a comma splice, and it is an error. You must separate the two independent clauses with a period or a semicolon, or you must add a coordinating conjunction after the comma (. . . , but . . .).

A transition is not enough to separate two sentences, either, even with a comma. You need to end the previous sentence:

NOT *The man bought a new car, however, his wife didn't know about it.

Summary of patterns:

```
NOT *S  +  V    S  +  V
NOT *S  +  V ,  S  +  V
NOT *S  +  V ,  transition, S  +  V
BUT  S  +  V .  S  +  V
OR   S  +  V ;  S  +  V
OR   S  +  V ,  conjunction S  +  V
OR   S  +  V .  Transition, S  +  V
OR   S  +  V ;  transition, S  +  V
```

Exercise 4

Identify the following student sentences as correctly formed (OK), a run-on sentence (RO), or a comma splice (CS).

1. It was close to 7 o'clock, I began to prepare dinner.
2. My grandparents have a small field they grow vegetables there.
3. It was mid-June when we went to Florida, we spent the whole summer there.
4. On the way back to the hotel, we went to visit Saranac Lake.
5. He picked the flowers, two hours later they died.

(See Answer Key, p. 154.)

D. Coordinate Tags

When *and* is used with *so* or *neither* in a coordinate tag, inverted word order (V + S) follows:

My sister likes swimming, *and so do I.*
My brother didn't go skiing last week, *and neither did I.*

(See also Troublespot 11, "Verb Forms.")

Editing Advice

If you want to check how a sentence you have written is connected to the ideas surrounding it, ask yourself these questions:

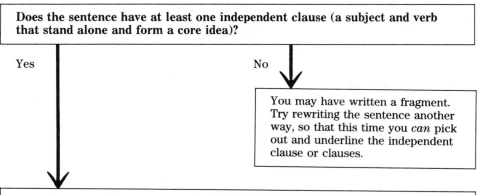

(Flowchart continued)

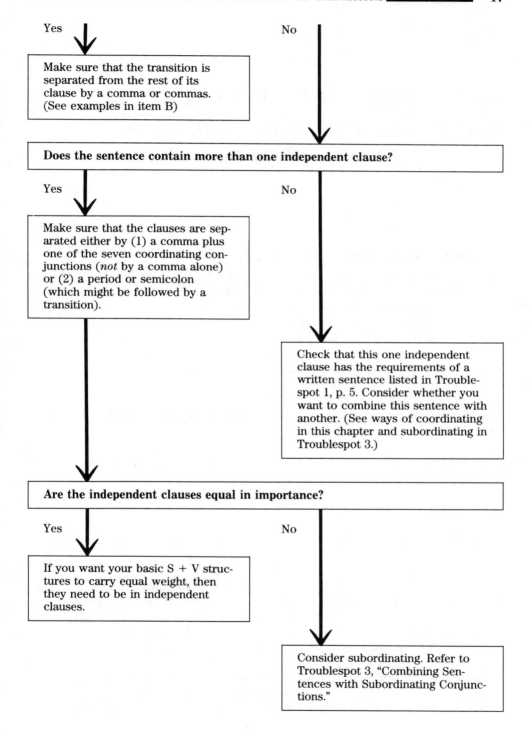

Yes

No

Make sure that the transition is separated from the rest of its clause by a comma or commas. (See examples in item B)

Does the sentence contain more than one independent clause?

Yes

No

Make sure that the clauses are separated either by (1) a comma plus one of the seven coordinating conjunctions (*not* by a comma alone) or (2) a period or semicolon (which might be followed by a transition).

Check that this one independent clause has the requirements of a written sentence listed in Troublespot 1, p. 5. Consider whether you want to combine this sentence with another. (See ways of coordinating in this chapter and subordinating in Troublespot 3.)

Are the independent clauses equal in importance?

Yes

No

If you want your basic S + V structures to carry equal weight, then they need to be in independent clauses.

Consider subordinating. Refer to Troublespot 3, "Combining Sentences with Subordinating Conjunctions."

TROUBLESPOT 3

Combining Sentences with Subordinating Conjunctions

A. Coordination and Subordination

You can combine two simple sentences by using coordinating conjunctions or transitions; the result is two independent clauses (see examples in Troublespot 2). You also have the option of making one of your independent ideas subordinate to (dependent on) the other.

Look at these two simple sentences:

Hemingway was a sentimental man.
He hardly ever threw anything away.

One way to combine these ideas is to coordinate the sentences (Troublespot 2) as follows:

Hemingway was a sentimental man, so he hardly ever threw anything away.

Another way is to provide a transition:

Hemingway was a sentimental man. In fact, he hardly ever threw anything away.

In the preceding examples, the two ideas have equal weight and, therefore, equal importance in the reader's mind. One way to change the emphasis is to subordinate one idea to the other: make the most important idea the independent clause and make the less important idea a *condensed phrase*, attaching it to the core idea. The following examples include condensed phrases:

Hemingway, *a sentimental man*, hardly ever threw anything away.
Being sentimental, Hemingway hardly ever threw anything away.
For sentimental reasons, Hemingway hardly ever threw anything away.

The two clauses can also be combined by keeping them as full clauses—(subject + verb) and (subject + verb)—but making one of them subordinate to the other by introducing it with a *subordinating conjunction;* for example:

> Hemingway, *who was a sentimental man,* hardly ever threw anything away.
> *Because Hemingway was a sentimental man,* he hardly ever threw anything away.

The dependent clause in each of these sentences is in italics. Note that it cannot stand alone. It has been made subordinate to the independent clause and is now dependent on it for meaning.

B. *Subordinating Conjunctions and Dependent Clauses*

The box on p. 20 shows both the relationships that allow one sentence to be subordinated to another (type of clause) and the subordinating conjunctions used to begin dependent clauses.

C. *Avoiding Fragments with Subordinate Clauses*

A subordinate clause cannot stand alone. The following excerpts from student writing are ungrammatical:

> *I went home early. Because I had a lot of work to do.
> *Although he arrived late for the interview. He got the job.
> *He bought a new car. Which was bright red.

A subordinate clause must be connected to an independent clause. When you begin a sentence with a subordinating conjunction like *because, if, although,* or *when,* look for the following pattern:

Subordinating conjunction	S	+	V	, S	+	V .
Although	he		arrived late,	he		got the job.

D. *Clauses with* Although

To show concession or unexpected result, use a subordinating conjunction like *although,* a coordinating conjunction like *but,* or a transition like *however.* Use only one of these.

DEPENDENT CLAUSES

Type of clause	Examples of subordinating conjunctions
Relative	that, who, whom, which, whose (*that, whom, which* are sometimes omitted as the object of the clause) The man *who* won the lottery bought a new car.
Time	when, before, after, until, since, as soon as *When* he won the money, he decided to buy a car.
Place	where, wherever She drove *wherever* she wanted.
Cause	because, as, since She got a parking ticket *because* she parked illegally.
Purpose	so that, in order that He drove fast *so that* he could get to work on time.
Result	so . . . that, such . . . that He drove *so* fast *that* he got a speeding ticket.
Condition	if, unless *If* she hadn't won the lottery, she would have been very unhappy.
Concession (unexpected result)	although, even though *Although* she thought she was a good driver, she got a lot of tickets for speeding.
Included statement or question	that (sometimes omitted), what, why, how, where, when, who, whom, which, whose, whether, if He knows *why* he gets so many tickets. He knows [that] his business will be successful.

> Although he studied hard, he failed the exam.
> He studied hard, but he failed the exam.
> He studied hard; however, he failed the exam.
> NOT *Although he studied hard, but he failed the exam.

Exercise 1

Connect or combine the following sentences in as many ways as possible. Indicate whether you are using a coordinating conjunction, a transition, or a subordinating conjunction.

Example:

Hemingway was a sentimental man.
He hardly ever threw anything away.

One student found six ways to connect and combine these two sentences:

Hemingway was a sentimental man, so he hardly ever threw anything
away. (coordinating conjunction)
Hemingway was a sentimental man. Consequently, he hardly ever threw
anything away. (transition)
Because (As, Since) Hemingway was a sentimental man, he hardly ever
threw anything away. (subordinating conjunction—cause)
Hemingway was such a sentimental man that he hardly ever threw anything away. (subordinating conjunction—result)
Hemingway was so sentimental that he hardly ever threw anything away.
(subordinating conjunction—result)
Hemingway, who was a sentimental man, hardly ever threw anything away.
(subordinating conjunction—relative)

1. Teachers say they want diligent students.
   What they really need is imaginative students.
2. I often arrive late.
   My boss gets very angry.
3. He won some money.
   He bought some new clothes.
4. Everyone in my family got sick.
   I didn't.
5. My sister didn't win the essay prize.
   She was proud of her work.
6. Prices went up.
   Demand went down.
7. She got her paycheck.
   She left for her vacation.
8. They were found guilty of robbery.
   They were sentenced to jail.
9. He made a lot of money for the company by his financial dealings.
   He was not promoted to vice-president.
10. He wasted many of the company's resources.
    There was hardly anything left.

(See Answer Key, p. 154.)

Exercise 2

Combine the following group of short sentences into one or two long sentences by using coordinating conjunctions, transitions, or subordinating conjunctions or by condensing ideas. Find as many ways to do this as you can.

> Jack wanted to make a good impression.
> Jack wore a suit.
> The suit was new.
> The suit belonged to his brother.
> Jack was the new head clerk.
> The suit was too big for him.
> The pants kept falling down.

(See Answer Key, p. 155.)

Exercise 3

This is how one student combined the seven sentences in Exercise 2 into a single sentence:

> Wanting to make a good impression, Jack, the new head clerk, wore his brother's new suit, but the suit was so big for him that the pants kept falling down.

Examine the structure of this new sentence by answering these questions:

1. How many independent clauses are there? What are they?
2. What is the subject and verb of each independent clause?
3. If there is more than one independent clause, how are the independent clauses connected?
4. How many subordinate clauses are there (a subject + verb combination preceded by a subordinating conjunction)?
5. How many other core ideas have been attached to the independent clause(s)?

(See Answer Key, p. 155.)

Examine the structure of some of the sentences you formed in Exercise 2 by asking the same questions.

Exercise 4

Find as many ways as you can to combine each of the following sentence groups into one sentence. Include all the ideas that are there, but collapse sentences into words or phrases if you wish. You may also add words (subordinating conjunctions, for example, or coordinating conjunctions like *and* and *but*) that will help you combine the ideas. Use the chart of subordinating conjunctions in item B to help you, too.

1. I watched a little girl.
   She was carrying a big shopping bag.
   I felt sorry for her.
   I offered to help.

2. My family was huge.
   My family met at my grandparents' house every holiday.
   There were never enough chairs.
   I always had to sit on the floor.

3. Computers save time.
   Many businesses are buying them.
   The managers have to train people to operate the machines.
   Sometimes they don't realize that.

4. All their lives they have lived with their father.
   Their father is a politician.
   He is powerful.
   He has made lots of enemies.

5. She wanted to be successful.
   She worked day and night.
   She worked for a famous advertising agency.
   Eventually she became a vice-president.

6. He really wants to go skiing.
   He has decided to go to a beach resort in California.
   His sister lives in the beach resort.
   He hasn't seen her for ten years.

(See Answer Key, p. 155.)
   Which sentence of each group did you select as the independent clause of your new sentence? Why did you select that one? How does the meaning of your sentence change if you choose a different independent clause?

Editing Advice

   Ask these questions about a piece of writing that you want to improve:

> **Are there any passages that seem choppy and disconnected because they consist of a lot of short sentences?**

Yes   No

(Flowchart continued)

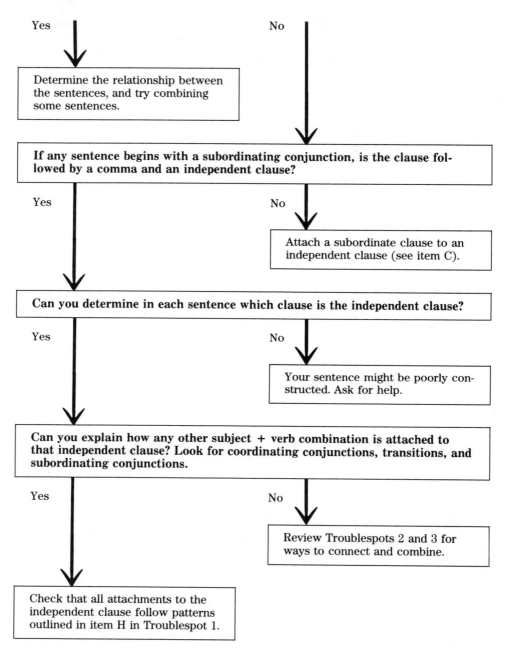

Yes | No

Determine the relationship between the sentences, and try combining some sentences.

If any sentence begins with a subordinating conjunction, is the clause followed by a comma and an independent clause?

Yes | No

Attach a subordinate clause to an independent clause (see item C).

Can you determine in each sentence which clause is the independent clause?

Yes | No

Your sentence might be poorly constructed. Ask for help.

Can you explain how any other subject + verb combination is attached to that independent clause? Look for coordinating conjunctions, transitions, and subordinating conjunctions.

Yes | No

Review Troublespots 2 and 3 for ways to connect and combine.

Check that all attachments to the independent clause follow patterns outlined in item H in Troublespot 1.

TROUBLESPOT 4

Punctuation

A. *End Punctuation*

The end of a sentence is signaled by a period (.), a question mark (?), or an exclamation point (!). Common sentence punctuation problems are illustrated in the accompanying box. See also Troublespot 1, item B; Troublespot 2, item C; and Troublespot 3, item C.

<table>
<tr><th colspan="3">PROBLEMS WITH END PUNCTUATION</th></tr>
<tr><th>Problem</th><th>Feature</th><th>Example</th></tr>
<tr>
<td>Run-on</td>
<td>No end punctuation

Transition: no end punctuation</td>
<td>*My sister is shy she doesn't say much.
*My brother works hard however he doesn't make a lot of money.</td>
</tr>
<tr>
<td>Comma splice</td>
<td>Comma separates two sentences with no coordinating conjunction
Comma separates two sentences with transition word</td>
<td>*My sister is shy, she doesn't say much.

*My brother works hard, however he doesn't make a lot of money.</td>
</tr>
<tr>
<td>Fragment</td>
<td>Sentence has no subject

No complete verb

No independent clause</td>
<td>*My boss is never late. Works extremely hard every day.
*Both of them working very hard.
*Because she wanted to save a lot of money to buy a car.
*Although he was offered a job in a new company, which was located in Florida.
*Hoping to get more money because he had a lot of bills to pay.</td>
</tr>
</table>

B. Semicolon

There are two main uses of the semicolon.

1. To signal the end of a sentence, in place of a period, when the meaning of the two sentences is very closely connected.

   He likes dogs a lot; he even has four in his small apartment.

2. To separate items in a list when commas are used elsewhere in the sentence.

   They bought a big ham, big enough to feed 12 people; a turkey, which they had to wheel home in a shopping cart; and 10 pounds of vegetables.

Compare this with

   They bought a ham, a turkey, and some vegetables. (See item C2.)

C. Comma

There are five main uses of commas:

1. To set off a phrase or clause before the subject

   While she was cooking, her friends arrived.

2. To separate items in a list when no other internal commas are used

   They bought lamps, chairs, and wastebaskets.

   Sometimes the last comma before *and* is omitted:

   They bought lamps, chairs and wastebaskets.

3. To indicate inserted material

   Harold, my boss, gave me a raise.

   Note that commas appear on both sides of the inserted material.
        Dashes (—) and parentheses ( ) also signal inserted material, telling the reader that the information is not essential but a kind of aside.

4. To introduce or end a quotation

   He said, "You've deserved it."
   "You've deserved it," he said.

5. To separate independent clauses joined with a coordinating conjunction

I was grateful, so I sent him a birthday gift.

Note that a comma is not used before a clause introduced by the subordinator *that:*

He said that she should not worry.
The book that you gave me is very interesting.

Exercise 1

Examine all the uses of commas in the following passage from an article called "Mr. Doherty Builds His Dream Life." Try to fit each comma use into one of the five categories in item C.

Example:

I'm not in E. B. White's class as a writer or in my neighbors' league as a farmer, but I'm getting by.

The comma separates independent clauses joined with a conjunction.

And after years of frustration with city and suburban living,① my wife

Sandy and I have finally found contentment here in the country.

It's a self-reliant sort of life. We grow nearly all of our fruits and veg-

etables. Our hens keep us in eggs,② with several dozen left over to sell each

week. Our bees provide us with honey,③ and we cut enough wood to just

about make it through the heating season.

It's a satisfying life too. In the summer we canoe on the river,④ go pic-

nicking in the woods and take long bicycle rides. In the winter we ski and

skate. We get excited about sunsets. . . .

But the good life can get pretty tough. Three months ago when it was

30 below,⑤ we spent two miserable days hauling firewood up the river on a

toboggan. Three months from now,[6] it will be 95 above and we will be cultivating corn,[7] weeding strawberries and killing chickens. Recently,[8] Sandy and I had to reshingle the back roof. Soon Jim,[9] 16,[10] and Emily,[11] 13,[12] the youngest of our four children,[13] will help me make some long-overdue improvements. . . .

(See Answer Key, p. 156.)

D. Colon

A colon introduces explanatory and listed items.

I need two new pieces of furniture: a dining table and a coffee table.

A colon often follows the phrase *as follows*. It is not used after *such as*. A colon can also be used to introduce a direct quotation:

I heard his angry words: "Get out!"

E. Apostrophe

An apostrophe is used in contracted forms, such as the following:

can't, won't, didn't, he's, she'd, they're, let's

However, these contractions are not usually used in formal academic writing.

An apostrophe is also used to signal possession or ownership. Add -'s to signal possession. If the noun is a plural form ending in -s, add only an apostrophe.

her son's room (one son)
her daughters' room (two daughters, one room)
the teachers' reports (more than one teacher: plural -s)
the children's books (more than one child, but no -s for plural form)

However, apostrophes are not used with the names of buildings, objects, or pieces of furniture (the hotel pool, the car door, the table leg) or with possessive adjectives (its, yours, hers). The form *it's* is a contraction for *it is* or *it has*.

Exercise 2

Rewrite the following phrases, using an apostrophe.

Example:

the bone belonging to the dog
the dog's bone

1. the toys belonging to the baby
2. the toys belonging to the babies
3. the problems of the teachers
4. the decision made by my family
5. the plans made by the women
6. the proposals offered by the politicians
7. the desk belonging to the secretary
8. the home belonging to the couple
9. the park belonging to the people
10. the ball belonging to the little boy

(See Answer Key, p. 156.)

F. *Quotation Marks*

For quotation marks, see Troublespot 20, "Quoting and Citing Sources."

Exercise 3

Punctuation marks have been removed from the following passage from an article called "The Analysts Who Came to Dinner." Add punctuation where it is appropriate.

The study also offers a clue to why middle children often seem to have a

harder time in life than their siblings Lewis found that in families with

three or four children dinner conversation tends to center on the oldest

child who has the most to talk about and the youngest who needs the

most attention Middle children are invisible says Lewis When you see

someone get up from the table and walk around during dinner chances are its the middle child There is however one great equalizer that stops all conversation and deprives everyone of attention When the TV is on Lewis says dinner is a non-event

Despite the feminist movement Lewiss study indicates that preparing dinner continues to be regarded as womans work even when both spouses have jobs. Some men do help out but for most husbands dinnertime remains a relaxing hour

(See Answer Key, p. 156, for the author's choices.)

Editing Advice

To check your punctuation, read your piece of writing slowly, and ask the following questions:

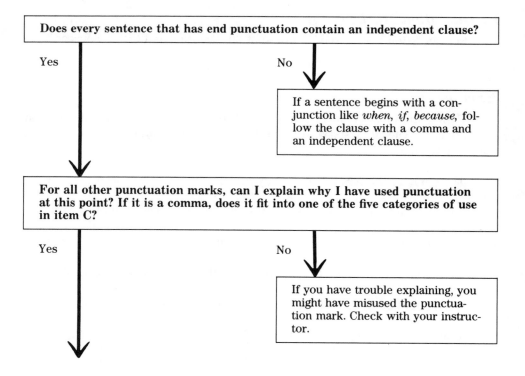

(Flowchart continued)

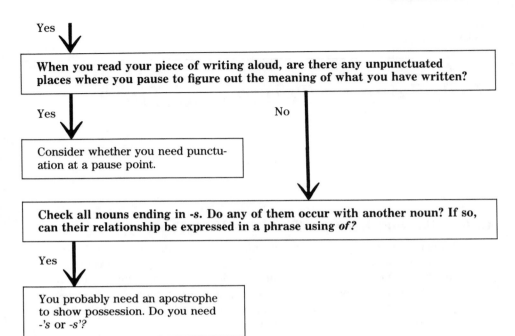

Yes ↓

When you read your piece of writing aloud, are there any unpunctuated places where you pause to figure out the meaning of what you have written?

Yes ↓   No

Consider whether you need punctuation at a pause point.

↓

Check all nouns ending in *-s*. Do any of them occur with another noun? If so, can their relationship be expressed in a phrase using *of?*

Yes ↓

You probably need an apostrophe to show possession. Do you need *-'s* or *-s'?*

TROUBLESPOT 5

Verb Tenses: Tense and Time

A. *Relationship Between Time and Verb Tense*

Choosing a verb tense means that you have to relate to time and the appropriate aspect of time. You begin by considering what time you are referring to—past, present, or future—and then you consider the relationship of that time to the action of the verb—progressive, perfect, or the combination of perfect progressive. For the most commonly used active-voice verb tenses, use the boxes (in items B through E) and examples to help you establish which time relationships you want to express. Troublespots 6 and 8 give more details about the difficulties that can occur with present-future and past tenses, respectively; active and passive forms are discussed in Troublespot 9 and modal auxiliaries in Troublespot 10. A verb form summary, with a one-page summary chart of the verb system, appears in Troublespot 11.

B. *Simple Tenses*

The simple tenses refer to a specific time in the past, a repeated action or a general truth in the present, and a specific time in the future.

Time Relationship Expressed: Simple		
Past	*Present*	*Future*
wrote	writes/write	will write
		am/is/are going to write
did _____ write?	does/do _____ write?	

Example:

She *wrote* a story yesterday. (completed in definite and known past time: for example, last week, a month ago, in 1990)

She *writes* every day. (repeated action or habit in present time: once a week, whenever she can, often)
She *writes* for a living. (general truth)
She *will write* to you next week. (future time stated; definite statement or promise)
She's *going to write* an article about child rearing. (implied future time; a plan)

Note: In clauses beginning with *when, before, after, until,* or *as soon as,* use the present and not the future tense for simple time:

When she *arrives,* we'll begin the meeting.

C. Progressive Tenses

Progressive tenses refer to an action that is in progress at a specified time. The *-ing* form of the main verb occurs with an auxiliary or auxiliaries (helping verbs like *was* and *will be*). The *-ing* form alone is not a complete verb.

Time Relationship Expressed: Progressive (In Progress at a Known Time)		
Past	*Present*	*Future*
was/were writing	am/is/are writing	will be writing

Example:

She *was writing* when I called her at 8 o'clock last night. (happening and continuing at a known or stated time in the past: I interrupted her; she probably continued afterward)
She *was writing* all day yesterday. (happening continuously over a long period of time in the past)
She *is writing* at this moment. (activity in present: now, right now)
She *will be writing* when you call her at 8 o'clock tonight. (happening at a known or stated time in the future: and she will probably continue writing after you call)

Note: The *-ing* form is not used for verbs expressing states of mind (such as *believe, know, understand, want, hate, seem, need*), senses *(taste, smell),* or possession *(have, own).* The simple forms are used instead. (See also Troublespot 6, item B4.)

D. Perfect Tenses

The perfect tenses indicate that an action has been completed, or *perfected*, before a known time or event. They are formed with the participle form of the main verb (often called the *past participle*, even though it does not always indicate past time).

Time Relationship Expressed: Perfect (Completed Before a Known Time or Event)		
Past	*Present*	*Future*
had written	has/have written	will have written

Example:

She *had* (already) *written* one story when she went to high school. (two past events indicated—an activity was completed by a stated time in the past: she wrote the story when she was 12, started high school when she was 14)

She *has* (already, just) *written* two stories. (activity completed some time before the present—the main point is not when she actually wrote them but that she *has written* them at some time in the past, with the effect being relative to present time)

She *will* (already) *have written* three stories when she graduates from high school next year. (two future events indicated—an activity will be completed by a stated time in the future: first she will write the stories; then she will graduate)

E. Perfect Progressive Tenses

These tenses are used to express how long an action or event continues and when it ends. Both the length of action and the time of its ending are stated or implied. Time expressions with *since* and *for* are frequently found with these tenses. The *-ing* form of the main verb is used.

Time Relationship Expressed: In Progress for a Stated Length of Time and up to a Known or Specific Time or Event		
Past	*Present*	*Future*
had been writing	has/have been writing	will have been writing

Example:

She *had been writing* for four hours before all the lights went out. (one event interrupted by the other; both the length of time and the end of the action in the past must be stated)

She *has been writing* a novel since 1987. (length of time stated or implied and continues until the present: she will probably continue; she has not finished the novel yet)

She *will have been writing* for six hours by the time the party starts at 8 o'clock tonight. (an event in the future interrupts or indicates the end of the action; both length of time and final event must be stated or clear from the context)

F. Consistency of Tenses

Consistency of tenses is important. Usually, the verb tenses a writer uses in a passage will fit consistently into one of two time clusters: past or present-future. The accompanying box summarizes the four tense-time relationships and divides them into two time clusters of verb forms that can occur in a piece of writing with no switch in time reference.

Tense-time Relationships		
Time relationship	*Past cluster*	*Present-future cluster*
Simple	wrote	writes/write will write
Progressive	was/were writing	am/is/are writing will be writing
Perfect	had written	has/have written will have written
Perfect progressive	had been writing	has/have been writing will have been writing

If the verb itself does not indicate the time cluster, the first auxiliary verb of the verb phrase will. The forms are shown in the following box.

Past and Present-future Forms of the First Auxiliary Verb	
Past	*Present-future*
was/were	am/is/are
did	does/do
had	has/have
would	will (would)
could	can (could)
should	shall (should)
might	may (might)
had to	has to/have to/must

Note that whereas modal forms like *will* and *can* are used only to indicate present-future time, forms like *would* and *could* can be used, in different contexts and with different meanings, in both time clusters.

Exercise 1

Do not surprise or confuse your reader by switching from one tense to another in the middle of a paragraph. If you do change tenses, be sure you have a good reason. In the following paragraph, for instance, the time switches from present-future to past at the point marked with an asterisk, but the reader is not surprised. Why not? What does the writer do to prepare us for the switch?

I think that big families can offer their members a lot of support. When a child has done something wrong, there is always someone to turn to. Or if he feels upset about a fight with a friend, even if his mother isn't at home, an aunt or a grandmother will be able to comfort him and offer advice. *Once when I was six years old, I fell off my bicycle. I had been riding very fast around the block in a race with my friends. My father was working and my mother was out shopping. But the house was still full of people; my aunt bathed my knees, my grandmother gave me a glass of milk and a cookie, and my uncle drove me to the doctor's office.

(See Answer Key, p. 156.)

Exercise 2

Read the following passage from "Mr. Doherty Builds His Dream Life" by Jim Doherty.

We love the smell of the earth warming and the sound of cattle lowing. We watch for hawks in the sky and deer in the cornfields.

But the good life can get pretty tough. Three months ago when it was 30 below, we spent two miserable days hauling firewood up the river on a toboggan. Three months from now, it will be 95 above and we will be cultivating corn, weeding strawberries and killing chickens. Recently, Sandy

and I had to reshingle the back roof. Soon Jim, 16, and Emily, 13, the

youngest of our four children, will help me make some long-overdue im-

provements on the privy that supplements our indoor plumbing when we

are working outside. Later this month, we'll spray the orchard, paint the

barn, plant the garden and clean the hen house before the new chicks

arrive.

Now underline each complete verb phrase and identify (1) which time cluster
(past or present-future) it fits into, (2) what time is expressed, and (3) what signals, if any, Doherty gives for any switches. Write a list of the verbs and your
identifications. For example, your first entry might read, "*love:* present; simple
tense."
(See Answer Key, p. 157.)

Exercise 3

Choose a passage from an article in a book, newspaper, or magazine. Underline the verbs, and identify what time is expressed according to the boxes in
items B through E.

Editing Advice

If you are having problems with verb tenses, look at all the active-voice
verbs in your draft, one paragraph at a time, and ask these questions:

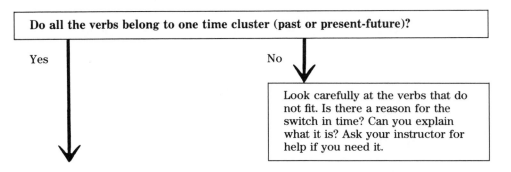

Do all the verbs belong to one time cluster (past or present-future)?

Yes

No

Look carefully at the verbs that do
not fit. Is there a reason for the
switch in time? Can you explain
what it is? Ask your instructor for
help if you need it.

(Flowchart continued)

Troublespot 5

Yes

Look at each verb again. Does the tense you have used match up exactly with one of the examples in items B through E? Does each verb convey precisely the time you had in mind, the relationship to other times or actions, and the idea of an action completed or in progress? (Refer to the examples with the verb *write*.)

No

Rewrite the verb so that it fits the examples and provides the appropriate indication of time. Ask for help if you need it.

TROUBLESPOT 6

Verb Tenses: Present-Future

A. *The Present-Future Cluster of Active Verbs*

The table on the following page shows the forms that commonly occur together when you write about present-future time. Sometimes present tenses are used to indicate future time, as in the following:

The train leaves early tomorrow morning.
She's going to China next year.

Some of the complexities of the tenses will be explained and illustrated in this troublespot.

B. *Simple Present*

The simple present tense is used for the following:

1. Habitual actions
    This is often used with *often, usually, frequently, sometimes,* and expressions such as *every day* or *every year.*

She writes to her brother once a month.

2. General truths

Water turns to ice when it freezes.
Most children play with blocks.
Parents make a lot of sacrifices for their children.

3. Future travel plans

He leaves at 6 o'clock tomorrow morning.

Active Verbs: Present-Future Cluster

Time reference	Present	Future
Simple	*main verb: present tense* She gets up at 6 A.M. *question: do/does + simple form* Does she get up early? *negative: do/does + simple form* They do not (don't) get up early.	*will + simple form* We will/won't leave soon. ALTERNATIVES *am/is/are going to + simple form* She's going to leave tomorrow. *main verb: basic present* We leave for France tomorrow. *main verb: progressive* I'm flying to Greece tomorrow.
Progressive	*am/is/are + -ing* He is leaving now.	*will be + -ing* She will be leaving soon.
Perfect	*has/have + participle* I have been to Europe. (at some time before now)	*will have + participle* I will have left by the time you arrive.
Perfect progressive	*has/have been + -ing* I have been living here for six years. (up until now)	*will have been + -ing* By next month, I will have been living here for exactly 20 years.
Modal reference		
See Troublespot 10	*will/would* *can/could* *shall/should* *may/might* *must/has to/have to* *ought to* } *+ simple form*	

4. An action in progress with "mental activity" verbs

Some verbs are not used with a progressive *-ing* form even when they refer to an activity in progress. These verbs are associated with mental rather than physical activity.

That book belongs to me.
She looks happy.

He wants to leave now.
This stew tastes good.
The park belongs to the city.

Some of the common mental activity verbs appear on the following list.

Mental Activity Verbs Not Used in the Progressive

Senses	*Possession*	*Preference and desire*
see	have	need
hear	own	want
smell	belong	prefer
taste		like
		love

Thoughts	*Inclusion*	*Appearance*
think	include	seem
know	contain	appear
believe	comprise	look
understand		

5. To refer to what an author says and does, even if the author is dead

   Hemingway writes about hunting and traditional male pastimes.

6. In subordinate clauses of time after such expressions as *when, before, after, until, as soon as,* and *by the time,* when used with a future tense in the independent clause

   When he arrives, I will leave.
   Before you go, I'll give you what I owe you.

C. Present Progressive

The present progressive is used for the following purposes:

1. To indicate an action that is in progress at the moment of speaking or writing

   He is wearing a new suit.
   They are trying to finish their work.

Note that an auxiliary form of the verb *be* is necessary to form a complete verb.

NOT*They trying to finish their work.

2. To emphasize that a state or action is not permanent

She is living in my apartment for a few weeks.

When no change is implied but a general truth is stated, use the simple present.

My brother lives in San Diego.

3. To indicate a future plan

He's flying to Ecuador next Tuesday.

Exercise 1

Select either the simple present or the present progressive form for the verbs in parentheses.

1. Most of the people in Korea (play) _____ a sport.
2. He (understand) _____ everything the teacher says.
3. When the party (end) _____, we'll all go home by bus.
4. His sister (go) _____ to work by train every day.
5. The boss (need) _____ more time to work on the project right now.
6. Her father (wear) _____ his winter coat today.
7. That old sweater (look) _____ new.
8. I'll wait for you until the movie (begin) _____.
9. Most students (make) _____ career plans before they graduate.
10. The students in my class this semester (make) _____ a lot of progress in learning English.

(See Answer Key, p. 157.)

D. Present Perfect

The present perfect tense causes language learners a lot of trouble because it includes a reference to past time, but its focus is more on the effects of the past state or action on present time. It is formed by a present form of *have* (*has* or *have* + the participle form). The present perfect tense is used in the following situations:

1. To indicate something that occurred at an unspecified and unimportant time in the past. What the speaker or writer wants to emphasize is that it happened at some time before now, but the exact time before now is not stated.

   Someone has left a coat on the back of the chair. (We see it now; we don't know when someone left it there.)
   Have you seen that movie yet? (We are not interested in exactly when the person saw the movie.)
   I've met him several times.
   I've been to the Grand Canyon.

   This is used with expressions like *already, yet, frequently,* and *often.*

2. To indicate a recent event, often used with *just.*

   I've just finished my homework.

3. To indicate that an activity began in the past and has continued until now. This is often used with *since* or *for.*

   We have known each other for a long time.
   I've had that tie since 1982.

   For action verbs, use the present perfect progressive.

   She has been cooking for the last three hours.

Exercise 2

In the following passage, H. L. Mencken discusses his job as journalist and book critic at the magazine *The American Mercury.* He tells about what he has done in the previous 8⅓ years that he has been editing and writing for the magazine. He does not tell us the exact time when all these things happened—and indeed, when they happened is not his point. He wants us to know only about the variety of things that he has done in that time. The passage is taken from his one-hundredth column for the magazine. Fill in the blanks with the present perfect tense of the given verbs.

In those eight and a third years I (serve) _____ four editors, not
①

including myself; I (grow) _____ two beards and (shave)
②

_____ them off; I (eat) _____ 3,086 meals; I (make)
③   ④

_____ more than \$100,000 in wages, fees, refreshers [additional
⑤

fees], tips and bribes; I (write) _____ 510,000 words about books
⑥

and not about books; . . . I (write) _____ and (publish)
⑦

_____ eight books and (review) _____ them all favor-
⑧   ⑨

ably; I (have) _____ seventeen proposals of marriage from lady
⑩

poets.

(See Answer Key, p. 157)

E. Present Perfect Progressive

The present perfect progressive tense emphasizes the length of time an activity is in progress. It implies that it began in the past, is still in progress, and will probably continue into the future.

I have been waiting for 15 minutes.
She has been working for Morgan Stanley since 1984.

Exercise 3

In the following sentences written by students, correct any errors in verb tenses.

1. He is working for Sony since he came to the United States.
2. Most of the children in my country are wearing a uniform to school.
3. A teacher doesn't want to have students in her class who had caused a lot of trouble.
4. In kindergarten, teachers usually are teaching students the alphabet and the spelling of simple words.
5. In the picture, the woman who sits in the middle looks like the most powerful member of the family.
6. We see a lot of changes in China because right now a lot of people trying hard to educate themselves.
7. This is the first time that my brother was in the hospital.
8. They are sitting in that restaurant for the last three hours.

9. They will start building a new house as soon as they will get a mortgage.
10. Most people are doing exercises after work.

(See Answer Key, p. 157.)

Exercise 4

In a book, newspaper, or magazine, find a picture of people engaged in an activity. Write a description of the picture for a student in your class. Use present tenses to describe what is happening in the picture as you are looking at it. Read your description aloud to a small group, who should all try to draw the scene that you describe.

Exercise 5

Describe the daily routine of someone in your family. Use the present simple tense and the present perfect where necessary.

Editing Advice

If you have problems with verb tenses, look at your piece of writing, underline the complete verb forms, and ask the following questions:

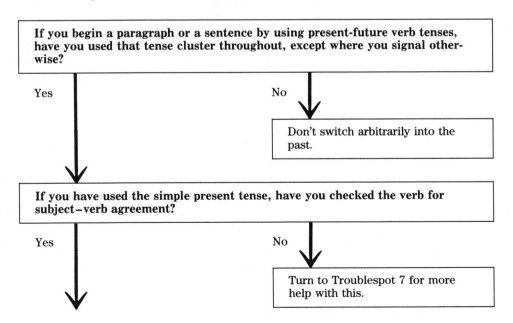

If you begin a paragraph or a sentence by using present-future verb tenses, have you used that tense cluster throughout, except where you signal otherwise?

Yes   No

Don't switch arbitrarily into the past.

If you have used the simple present tense, have you checked the verb for subject–verb agreement?

Yes   No

Turn to Troublespot 7 for more help with this.

(Flowchart continued)

Troublespot 6

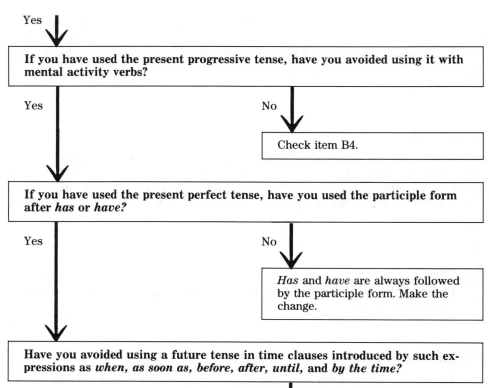

Yes

If you have used the present progressive tense, have you avoided using it with mental activity verbs?

Yes   No

Check item B4.

If you have used the present perfect tense, have you used the participle form after *has* or *have?*

Yes   No

Has and *have* are always followed by the participle form. Make the change.

Have you avoided using a future tense in time clauses introduced by such expressions as *when, as soon as, before, after, until,* and *by the time?*

No

See item B6, and make the change to the simple present or the present perfect.

TROUBLESPOT 7

Agreement

A. *Singular or Plural?*

Determining singular or plural endings can be confusing because an -*s* ending on a noun indicates plural (the *they* form), whereas an -*s* ending on a verb indicates singular (the *he/she/it*) form.

> The dog bark*s* every night. (*Dog* = *it*, so the verb is singular.)
> The dog*s* bark every night. (*Dogs* = *they*, so the verb is plural.)

Once again, the core of a sentence, S + V, is crucial for successful editing. In a clause or a sentence in the present tense, the verb has to agree in number with its subject—specifically with the head word (the most important word) of its subject, even if plural nouns occur in a phrase between the head word and the verb:

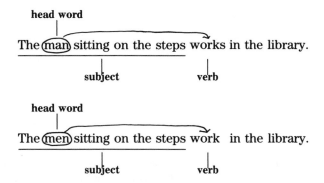

If the head word is a *he/she/it* form, use the third person singular form (-*s* ending) of the verb. If the head word is a *they* form, use the plural form of the verb (the simple form with no -*s* ending). If a subject is followed by more than one present tense verb, all forms must be parallel, and all must show agreement.

She <u>bakes</u> bread, <u>takes</u> music lessons, and <u>does</u> research.
They <u>work</u> hard and <u>earn</u> enough money.

Exercise 1

Read the following excerpt from "Mr. Doherty Builds His Dream Life."

Sandy, meanwhile, pursues her own hectic rounds. Besides the usual household routine, she oversees the garden and beehives, bakes bread, cans and freezes, chauffeurs the kids to their music lessons, practices with them, takes organ lessons on her own, does research and typing for me, writes an article herself now and then, tends the flower beds, stacks a little wood and delivers the eggs.

Underline all the verbs. How would the passage change if the writer were telling us not just about Sandy but about Sandy and her sister? Begin with "Sandy and her sister, meanwhile, pursue . . ." and write the new version.

(See Answer Key, p. 157.)

B. Verbs That Show Agreement

Agreement in number occurs with verbs used without auxiliaries in the present simple tense and with the following auxiliaries: *am/is/are; was/were; do/ does; has/have.*

Look at the following sentences:

The river was thawing.
The rivers have dried up.
Acid rain causes many problems.
Those people don't work here anymore.
Does his wife want to go?
My mother and I want to live together.

Auxiliaries like *will, would, can, could, shall, should, may, might,* and *must* do not change. In addition, they are always, whatever the subject, followed by the simple form of the verb:

The river might freeze.
The streams will probably freeze, too.

C. Subjects with Singular Verbs

Some words that regularly require a singular verb are troublesome to second-language students: *each, every, everyone, everybody, someone, somebody, anyone, anybody, no one, nobody, something.* In addition, the following words are singular: *-ing* forms; some nouns ending in *-s*, such as *news, physics, measles, politics,* and *series;* and subject clauses beginning with *what.*

Everyone wants to be liked.
Somebody who is standing over there wants to speak next.
Driving on icy roads is dangerous.
Politics interests me a lot.
What they want to do is start their own business.

Look for examples of these when you read, and note the verb form used.

D. Agreement with There in Subject Position

When a sentence starts with *There* plus a form of *be,* the verb agrees with the head word of the phrase that follows the verb.

There is one *bottle* on the table.
There are two *bottles* on the table.
There is some *wine* on the table.
There is a *vase* of flowers on the table.

You need to determine if the head word is singular or plural. Uncountable nouns are singular. See also Troublespot 12, "Nouns and Quantity Words."

There are a lot of *people* in the room.
There is a lot of *money* in my bag.

Exercise 2

Decide whether to use *is* or *are* in the following sentences.

1. There _____ some apples in the bowl on the table.
2. There _____ some money in my wallet.
3. There _____ a carton of milk in the refrigerator.
4. There _____ a box of books in the basement.
5. There _____ a lot of voters in rural regions.
6. There _____ a lot of food on the shelves.

7. There _____ a few coffee cups in the dishwasher.
8. There _____ no knives in the drawer.
9. There _____ no furniture in the room.
10. There _____ many serious problems that the voters in this district have to face.

(See Answer Key, p. 158.)

E. Compound Subjects

When a sentence has a compound subject (more than one subject), the verb must be plural in form.

My sister *visits* me every year. (subject: sister)
My aunt and my sister *visit* me every year. (compound subject: aunt and sister)

When the subject is formed with *either . . . or* or *neither . . . nor*, the verb agrees with the phrase closest to it.

Either her brothers or her father *has* the money.
Neither her mother nor her sisters *have* the money.

F. Agreement in Relative Clauses

When you write a relative clause beginning with *who, which,* or *that,* look for its *referent*—the word that *who, which,* or *that* refers to. The referent determines whether the verb should be singular or plural.

The *people* in my class *who are* studying English *do* a lot of extra reading.
The *student* in my class *who is* sitting in the corner usually *does* a lot of extra reading.

See also Troublespot 18, "Relative Clauses."

G. One Of

Beware! *One of* is followed by a plural noun and a singular verb, agreeing with the head word *one.*

One of her sons helps on the farm.

H. Some, Most, Any, All, None

Quantity words like *some, most, any, all,* and *none* are used in the following pattern, using a plural verb form with plural countable nouns and a singular verb form with uncountable nouns.

Most of the *students are* studying English.
Most of the *furniture is* very old.

With *none*, however, usage varies, and the following forms can both be found:

None of the books she took out of the library *was* interesting.
None of the books she took out of the library *were* interesting.

Exercise 3

Insert the correct form of the given verb in the following sentences.

1. One of the students in my class (come) _____ from Bangladesh.
2. The people who have invited me to the opening of the exhibition (want) _____ me to write an article about it afterward.
3. Almost everyone in my class (have) _____ a part-time job.
4. Writing essays (require) _____ a lot of skill.
5. Neither his wife nor his children (know) _____ that he has lost his job.
6. Every book that is assigned for this course (cost) _____ more than $20.
7. The president and his wife (have) _____ agreed to attend the ceremony.
8. My sister always (try) _____ her hardest.
9. Today's news (be) _____ surprising.
10. The bunch of flowers that she (want) _____ to buy (be) _____ very expensive.

(See Answer Key, p. 158.)

Editing Advice

If you have a problem with agreement of subject and verb, look at each troublesome verb you have written, and ask the following questions:

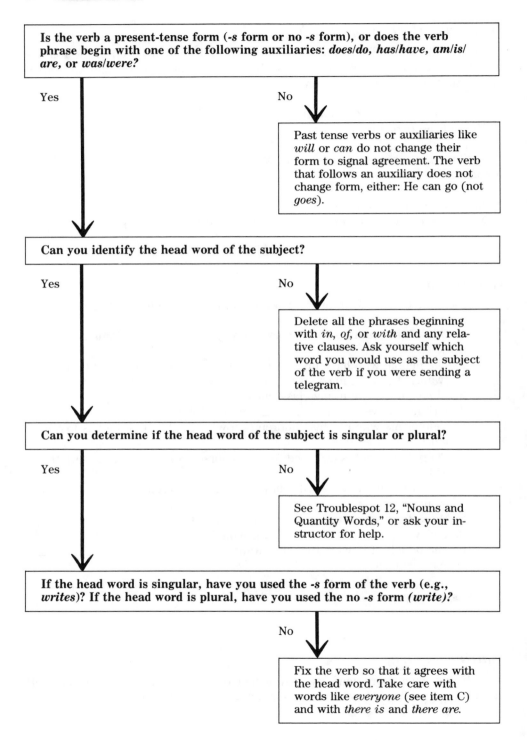

Is the verb a present-tense form (*-s* form or no *-s* form), or does the verb phrase begin with one of the following auxiliaries: *does/do, has/have, am/is/ are,* or *was/were?*

Yes

No

Past tense verbs or auxiliaries like *will* or *can* do not change their form to signal agreement. The verb that follows an auxiliary does not change form, either: He can go (not *goes*).

Can you identify the head word of the subject?

Yes

No

Delete all the phrases beginning with *in, of,* or *with* and any relative clauses. Ask yourself which word you would use as the subject of the verb if you were sending a telegram.

Can you determine if the head word of the subject is singular or plural?

Yes

No

See Troublespot 12, "Nouns and Quantity Words," or ask your instructor for help.

If the head word is singular, have you used the *-s* form of the verb (e.g., *writes*)? If the head word is plural, have you used the no *-s* form *(write)?*

No

Fix the verb so that it agrees with the head word. Take care with words like *everyone* (see item C) and with *there is* and *there are.*

TROUBLESPOT 8

Verb Tenses: Past

Exercise 1

The following passage uses verb forms of the present-future cluster.

Most of the students in my English class have a lot of work to do. They are taking four or five courses, and many of them work at full-time jobs as well so that they will be able to pay for their tuition, books, and living expenses. When they arrive home, all they want to do is sleep, but instead they have to do all the homework assignments. Many of them have come from other countries, so they are also trying to adjust to a new language and a new culture. They are all optimistic and think that they will succeed in spite of the difficulties.

Rewrite the passage with a new beginning: Last semester, most of the students in my English class . . . Underline each verb you changed.

(See Answer Key, p. 158.)

A. The Past Cluster of Active Verbs

The table on the following page shows the forms that commonly occur together when you write about past time.

Note that when the first verb of a sequence of complete verbs in a passage refers to past time, then as long as there is no indicated time change, the other verbs will also be in the past cluster.

He *explained* that he *had* just *returned.*
She *said* that she *would help* me.

Active Verbs: Past Cluster

Time reference	Past verb

Simple	past tense:
	    She *left* early.
	question and negative: *did* + simple form:
	    Did she *leave* early?
	    She *didn't leave* early.

Progressive	*was/were* + *-ing* They *were leaving* when I arrived.
Perfect	*had* + participle When I arrived, everyone *had left*.
Perfect progressive	*had been* + *-ing* We *had been trying* to call you for an hour before you called us.

Modal reference	
See Troublespot 10	would, could, should, might, had to + simple form would have, could have, should have, might have + participle

Exercise 2

For each of the verbs that you changed and underlined in Exercise 1, identify the time it refers to—simple past, past perfect, past progressive, past perfect
progressive, or modal past.

(See Answer Key, p. 158.)

B. Simple Past

The simple past tense is used when we state or imply that an event occurred at a specified time in the past.

They *walked* home last night because they *wanted* some exercise.

Regular verbs form the past tense by adding *-d* or *-ed* to the stem of the verb.
Many verbs have irregular past tense forms, such as *take—took*.

Last Tuesday, she *took* a taxi home.

The simple past is the tense commonly used to tell a story. It occurs often
in expository writing when a writer supports a generalization with an example or
an incident.

Most people tell white lies, even those who regard themselves as
very honest. Only a few days ago, my sister, for example, who is basically

a very moral person, told our parents that she was going to the library. In fact, she went to a party.

Exercise 3

Use one of the following passages to write a paragraph containing examples of past cluster verbs.

1. Cultural differences can cause problems. For example, once I . . .
2. The problems in my neighborhood are increasing. Last week, for instance, . . .
3. Even in a busy city, people find time for acts of kindness. A while ago, I . . .

C. Past Perfect

The past perfect (*had* + participle) is used only when a clear relationship exists with an event in simple past time. It indicates that an action was completed before another one in the past.

Yesterday I went to the library. I had never used a computer terminal before.

Note the time differences in these two sentences:

When I arrived at the party at 9 P.M., everyone had left. (The room was empty.)
When I arrived at the party at 9 P.M., everyone left. (They saw me and left!)

The past perfect is not used for simultaneous activities.

When I arrived in my country, I felt very happy.

It is not used for a single past activity.

Yesterday, I went to the library.

D. Past Progressive and Past Perfect Progressive

The past progressive tells about an action in progress at a specified time in the past.

When I arrived at the party at 9 P.M., everyone was leaving. (They were putting on their coats.)

Or it describes an activity in progress for a period of time in the past.

He was working while I was playing tennis.

The past perfect progressive (*had been* + *-ing*) tells us about the length of the action and the specific point when it ended. It occurs frequently with *since* or *for* to specify the duration of the action.

I had been playing for two hours when I fell and twisted my ankle.

Exercise 4

In the passage, insert appropriate past cluster forms of the verbs in parentheses. Add auxiliaries where necessary.

When I (be) _____ a little girl, every day my mother (take) _____
① ②

me to my grandmother's house and I (spend) _____ all day with her
③

and my cousins. We (play) _____ and (grow) _____ up together. We
④ ⑤

(know, not) _____ as many children as those in kindergarten, but we
⑥

(enjoy) _____ ourselves a lot and (learn) _____ how to be a really
⑦ ⑧

close family. One day, when we (play) _____ by the river, my cousin
⑨

(fall) _____ in the water, and my grandmother (have) _____ to
⑩ ⑪

jump in and pull him out. He (try) _____ to catch a butterfly when his
⑫

foot (slip) _____ and he suddenly (disappear)_____. My grand-
⑬ ⑭

mother (say) _____ that she (forget, never) _____ it, and she never
⑮ ⑯

(do)_____.
⑰

(See Answer Key, p. 158.)

Exercise 5

Select a photograph from your own collection. Write about your memories of the occasion beginning with "When _____ took this photograph, I . . ." Then go on to tell your readers interesting details about the event in the photograph. (For example, why was the baby crying? What was your sister wearing on her head? What was your brother doing? Why was your grandmother so unhappy?) Remember, since the photograph was taken in the past, you are writing about a past event.

E. *Past Time Structures:* Used to *and* Would

Used to and *would* tell about regular occurrences in the past. They tell about customs, habits, and rituals. Frequently, a narrative will begin with *used to* + simple form and then continue with *would* + simple form.

> When I lived in China, I *used to walk* three miles to school every day.
> I *would get up* at 5 A.M. and *would take* my breakfast bowl with me.

Editing Advice

To check your past cluster verb forms (active voice), ask the following questions about a piece of writing:

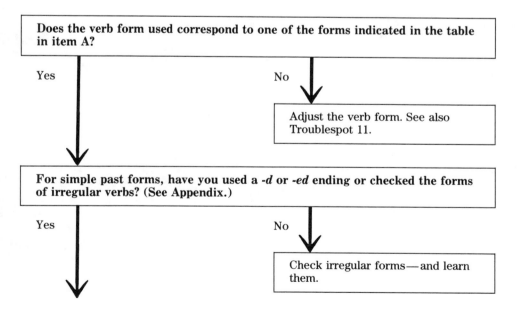

Does the verb form used correspond to one of the forms indicated in the table in item A?

Yes   No

Adjust the verb form. See also Troublespot 11.

For simple past forms, have you used a *-d* or *-ed* ending or checked the forms of irregular verbs? (See Appendix.)

Yes   No

Check irregular forms—and learn them.

(Flowchart continued)

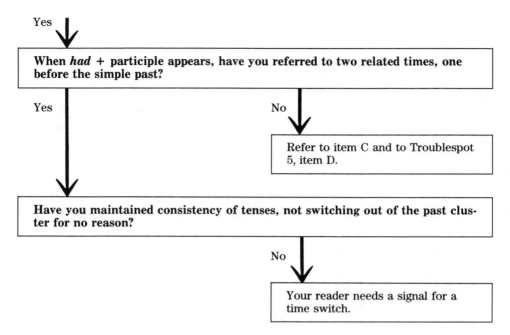

Yes

When *had* + participle appears, have you referred to two related times, one before the simple past?

Yes

No

Refer to item C and to Troublespot 5, item D.

Have you maintained consistency of tenses, not switching out of the past cluster for no reason?

No

Your reader needs a signal for a time switch.

TROUBLESPOT 9

Active and Passive

A. *Active and Passive*

The following sentence contains a verb in the active voice:

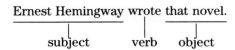

We can change the emphasis by rewriting the sentence like this:

That novel was written by Ernest Hemingway.

Note what we have done:

> We have reversed the order of the subject and object of the original sentence.
> We have changed the verb form to a form of *be* followed by the participle (see also Troublespot 11, "Verb Forms").
> We have added *by* before the original subject.

B. *Uses of the Passive*

Sometimes writers overuse the passive voice, which makes their writing flat and dull. But there are times when the passive is necessary to convey your meaning. Use the passive when it is not important to emphasize or even mention the doer of the action (sometimes called the *agent*).

> Good! The garbage *has been collected.*
> He *was promoted* to vice-president a month ago.
> When gold *was discovered* in the area, new towns sprang up overnight.
> Her performance *is being watched* very closely.

These tomatoes *were grown* in New Jersey.
I *was told* to send the form to you. (The writer doesn't want to say who did the telling.)

If the agent is important, the active voice is usually preferable.

Two prospectors discovered gold in the area.
NOT Gold was discovered in the area by two prospectors.
(But see #4 below.)

The passive voice occurs frequently in the following instances:

1. In scientific writing

The experiment was performed in 1983.

2. In journalism, or other writing, when the writer cannot or does not want to identify the agent

Jewelry worth $500,000 was stolen from the Hotel Eldorado late last night.

3. When the action is more important than who did it

In the 1980s, a lot of tall buildings were built in the middle of the city.

4. In a sentence with the same subject as the previous clause, when the flow of the sentences makes the passive acceptable

In the 1980s, a lot of tall buildings appeared in the city. They were built to provide more office space.
She stared at the chair. That old wooden rocking chair had been made by her father.

C. Forms of the Passive

The form and sequence of passive verbs is often a problem for students writing in a second language. Look at the examples on the following list.

Active	*Passive*
They paint the house every three years.	The house *is painted* every three years.

They painted the house last year.	The house *was painted* last year.
They will paint the house next year.	The house *will be painted* next year.
They are painting the house now.	The house *is being painted* now.
They were painting the house all last week.	The house *was being painted* all last week.
They have just painted the house.	The house *has just been painted.*
They had just painted the house when the roof collapsed.	The house *had just been painted* when the roof collapsed.
They will have painted the house by next Tuesday.	The house *will have been painted* by next Tuesday.

Note that in all the passive sentences, we use a form of *be* plus a participle. In addition, a *be* form can be preceded by modal auxiliaries (see Troublespot 10).

The house *should be painted.*
The house *might have been painted* last year; I'm not sure if it was.

D. Being *and* Been

Language learners sometimes get confused with the forms *been* and *being* because both are used in passive verbs and because pronunciation can blur a clear distinction. Remember the following:

Being is used after forms of *be* in passive verbs only.
Been is used after forms of *have* in both active and passive verbs.

Note the patterns:

(be) + *being* + participle (passive)

(have) + *been* + *-ing* (active)
  + participle (passive)

He *is being questioned* now. (He's being questioned.)
He *has been working* hard all day. (He's been working.)
He *has been taken* to the hospital. (He's been taken.)

E. Passive Idioms with Get and Have

Passives are sometimes formed with *get*.

She *got fired* last week.

This is informal usage; it is not appropriate for formal academic writing. Use "She was fired" instead.

Get and *have* are also used in a causative sense. The sentence

He washed the car.

does not mean the same as

He had the car washed.
OR He got the car washed.

In the first sentence, he did the washing himself. In the other two sentences, he paid or asked somebody to do it for him.

Exercise 1

Read the following passages, and write down all the verbs used as complete verb forms in independent and dependent clauses. Then indicate which verbs are active and which are passive.

1. If the nations of the world take immediate action, the destruction of the global environment can be slowed substantially. But . . . even if fossil-fuel emissions are cut drastically, the overall level of carbon dioxide in the atmosphere will still increase—along with the likelihood of global warming. Even if toxic dumping is banned outright and that ban is strictly enforced, some lakes and aquifers will be tainted by poisons that have already been released. (Philip Elmer-Dewitt, "Preparing for the Worst."

2. They were taught to keep their elbows close to their sides while cutting meat, and to hold the utensils in the tips of their fingers. They resisted the temptation to sop up the gravy with a piece of bread, and they made sure to leave a little of everything. (Evan S. Connell, *Mrs. Bridge.*

(See Answer Key, p. 159.)

Exercise 2

The following sentences all have a very general subject. Rewrite the sentences using the passive voice so that you emphasize what happened to what. Retain the time reference and tense that the original sentence expresses.

Example:

They have translated the book into 14 languages.
The book *has been translated* into 14 languages.

1. They have made a lot of changes in the curriculum.
2. They have canceled some popular courses.
3. They grow a lot of rice in Japan.
4. They are questioning the suspect right now.
5. They will revise the budget within the next few months.

(See Answer Key, p. 159.)

Editing Advice

When you want to examine closely whether you have correctly used a verb in the passive voice, ask these questions:

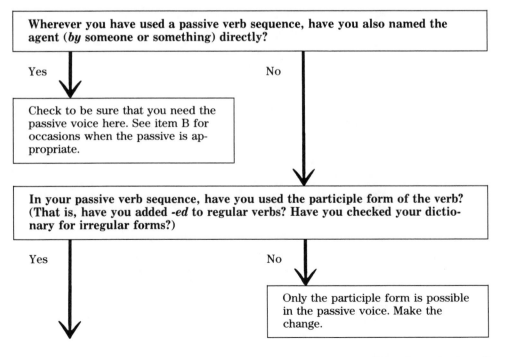

Wherever you have used a passive verb sequence, have you also named the agent (*by* someone or something) directly?

Yes

No

Check to be sure that you need the passive voice here. See item B for occasions when the passive is appropriate.

In your passive verb sequence, have you used the participle form of the verb? (That is, have you added *-ed* to regular verbs? Have you checked your dictionary for irregular forms?)

Yes

No

Only the participle form is possible in the passive voice. Make the change.

(Flowchart continued)

Yes

Does the verb phrase you have used include in its sequence a form of *be*, such as *is, was, were, are being, have been, will be, might be,* or *should have been?*

No

Check the examples of passive verbs in item C. Your verb sequence should correspond to one of those.

TROUBLESPOT 10

Modal Auxiliaries

A. *Modal Auxiliaries: Form and Meaning*

Be, have, and *do* are the auxiliaries used to form the various verb tenses of active and passive verbs, but other auxiliaries can also be used to supply additional meaning, such as that of ability *(can, could)*, advisability *(should)*, and necessity *(must/has to/have to/had to)*.

The features of modal auxiliaries are these:

1. They are followed by the simple form of the verb.

2. When the following simple form is *be* or *have*, an appropriate verb form follows (see Troublespot 11, "Verb Forms").

   He might be sleeping. (active)
   They should be reprimanded. (passive)
   He should have gone. (active)

3. They have only one form to indicate present time. They never add the *-s* ending.

   He can swim.
   They can swim.

This troublespot provides examples of the most common modal auxiliaries.

B. *The Uses of* Would

The table at the top of the next page shows the uses of the modal auxiliary *would*.

Uses of *Would*

Meaning	Past	Present-future
Polite question or statement		Would you help me? I would like your help.
Permission	Would you have minded if I had left?	Would you mind if I left now?
Past action, repeated (See Troublespot 8.)	Whenever I saw him, I would cry.	
Preference	I would rather have gone to the theater.	I would rather go to the movies than the theater. I'd rather not see that play.
Hypothetical condition (See Troublespot 19.)	I would have won if . . .	I would win if . . .

Exercise 1

In one sentence, state a preference using *would rather* and explain why in a clause beginning with *because*.

Example:

play tennis / go bowling
I'd rather play tennis than go bowling because I like to be outdoors.

1. work for myself / work for a big company
2. read a mystery story / read a biography
3. spend money on a vacation / pay to have my apartment painted
4. watch sports / play a game
5. go to the movies / have a picnic in the park

C. Expressing Ability and Permission

The table on p. 67 shows examples of modal auxiliaries that express ideas of ability and permission. Both past and present-future clusters are shown where they exist, and forms closely related to the modals in meaning are also included.

Modal Auxiliaries: Ability and Permission

Meaning	Past	Present-future
Ability	He knew he could win. She couldn't solve the problem. She was able to convince her boss to promote her. We could have won (if) . . . (But we didn't.)	She can speak French. She will be able to get a job in Paris next year. We could begin (if) . . . (See Troublespot 19.)
Permission	She said I could join the class. She said we were allowed to join the class.	May I join this class? You may/may not leave. Can I join this class? (less formal than *may*) Would you mind if I joined this class? (polite) Would you mind my joining this class? (polite and formal) Are we permitted (allowed) to join this class?

D. *Expressing Advisability*

The following table shows modal auxiliaries that express the idea of advisability.

Modal Auxiliaries: Advisability

Meaning	Past	Present-future
Advisability	*Advisable action didn't occur* We should have sent some flowers. (But we didn't.) We shouldn't have sent wine. (But we did.) We ought to have sent chocolates, too. *Advisable action might have occurred* We'd better not have made a mistake.	We should send some flowers. We shouldn't send wine. We ought to send chocolates, too. We had better be careful. (The result will be bad otherwise.) We had better not make a mistake.

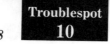
Note the form *should have* + participle:

should have gone
should have seen
should have taken

In speech, this is often abbreviated to *should've:*

We should've left earlier.

The following sentence is wrong:

*We should of left earlier.

It probably occurs because of the similarity between the pronunciation of *'ve* and *of.*

Exercise 2

Work with a partner. Each of you will write a letter stating a problem and asking for advice, ending with "What should I do?" or "What should I have done?" Exchange letters, and write a reply to each other, giving advice and using modal auxiliaries.

Modal Auxiliaries: Necessity, No Necessity, and Prohibition

Meaning	*Past*	*Present-future*
Necessity	The information had to make sense.	The information must make sense. The information has to make sense. The information will have to make sense. I have got to leave now. (informal) I've got to leave now. (informal; pronounced "I've gotta" or "I gotta")
	Last year, we were obliged to work every weekend.	We are obliged to work on weekends.
No necessity	You didn't have to leave so early.	You don't have to leave yet. It's still early. You won't have to leave early. You need not leave so early.
Prohibition	You weren't allowed to go in there!	You must not leave yet. There's still a lot of work to do. You're not allowed to leave yet. You won't be allowed to leave early.

E. Expressing Necessity, No Necessity, and Prohibition

The table on p. 68 shows the forms that we use to express the ideas of necessity, absence of necessity, and prohibition.

F. Expressing Expectation, Possibility, and Logical Deduction

The following table shows the forms used to express the ideas of expectation, possibility, and logical deduction.

Note the following distinction:

They *may be* leaving soon. (modal + simple form)
Maybe they are on their way. (*maybe* = perhaps)

Modal Auxiliaries: Expectation, Possibility, and Logical Deduction

Meaning	Past	Present-future
Expectation	We should have/ought to have received the package by now. (But we have not yet received it.)	We should/ought to receive the package today.
	He was supposed to make a speech last night.	He is supposed to make a speech at the banquet tomorrow.
Possibility	They may have/might have changed the test date.	They may/might increase tuition charges.
Logical deduction (more certain than *may/might*)	They must have changed the date.	There's no answer. He must be out.

Exercise 3

Write a paragraph in which you speculate about what your life might be like 20 years from now. Tell your readers what you think is possible and what your expectations are.

Exercise 4

Identify the difference in meaning among the sentences in the following groups. Suggest a situation in which each sentence might be used.

Example: She had to go to the dentist. (It was necessary; she had a very severe toothache.)

1. (a) You mustn't use the computer.
   (b) You don't have to use the computer.
2. (a) You should send in a photograph.
   (b) You have to send in a photograph.
3. (a) His experimental results might be challenged.
   (b) His experimental results must be challenged.
   (c) His experimental results should be challenged.
   (d) His experimental results should have been challenged.
4. (a) She should have saved a lot of money.
   (b) She might have saved a lot of money.
   (c) She must have saved a lot of money.
   (d) She didn't have to save a lot of money.
   (e) She had to save a lot of money.
5. (a) She had to see a therapist.
   (b) She had better see a therapist.
   (c) She didn't have to see a psychiatrist.

(See Answer Key, p. 159.)

Editing Advice

To check your use of modal auxiliaries in a piece of writing, ask the following questions:

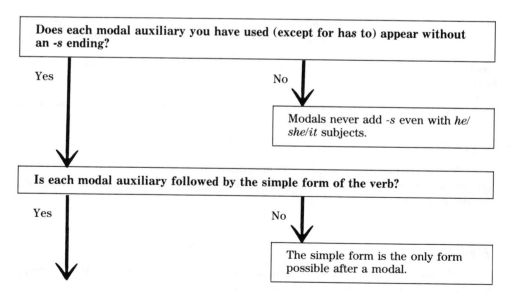

Does each modal auxiliary you have used (except for has to) appear without an -s ending?

Yes   No

Modals never add -s even with *he/she/it* subjects.

Is each modal auxiliary followed by the simple form of the verb?

Yes   No

The simple form is the only form possible after a modal.

(Flowchart continued)

Yes

Does the modal auxiliary fit with the time context of your piece of writing (present-future: *can, may, must, has to, have to;* past: *could, might, had to, would, would have, should have*)?

No

Check the tables in this troublespot to make sure you have used the correct form.

Verb Forms

A. Auxiliaries and Verb Forms

Verbs have five forms:

Simple (no -s)	-s	-ing	Past	Participle
paint	paints	painting	painted	painted
sing	sings	singing	sang	sung
take	takes	taking	took	taken

There are regular rules about which verb forms are used with which auxiliary verbs to form a complete verb in a clause or sentence. There are no exceptions. So choose which verb form to use according to the auxiliary verb you use. In the chart, "Verb Forms," p. 73, note that *only* the shaded forms of the verb are possible after the auxiliary verbs listed in the left-hand column.

You see from the "Verb Forms" chart that for most auxiliary sequences, the form of the verb after an auxiliary is fixed. You do not have to guess which form to use. Only with the *be* forms do you have a choice: you need to determine whether you want an active or a passive form before you decide whether to use the *-ing* or the participle form.

Exercise 1

In the following passages, underline each complete verb form. As you do so, refer to the "Verb Forms" chart, and note where each verb phrase fits in.

1. Christmas in America is said to be a holiday for children, but as I experienced the celebration of this holiday for the first time, it appeared to be more of a time for adults. The McKnights were planning to give a party and had invited me to go with them to the parties of

Verb Forms

I. Verb form used after an auxiliary

	Simple (no -s)	-s	-ing	Past	Participle
DO does/do did	▓				
WILL will/would can/could shall/should may/might must/ought to has to/have to/had to	▓				
HAVE has/have/had will have/would have can have/could have shall have/should have may have/might have must have/ought to have					▓

BE
am/is/are/was/were
has been/have been/had been
will be/would be
can be/could be
shall be/should be
may be/might be/must be
will have been/would have been
can have been/could have been
shall have been/should have been
may have been/might have been/
  must have been/ought to have
  been
			▓		Passive (see p. 59)

BEING am/is/are being was/were being					Passive (see p. 59)

II. Verb form used with no auxiliary

	Simple (no -s)	-s	-ing	Past	Participle
Simple time (past)				▓	
Simple time (present) (he, she, it forms as subject)		▓			
Simple time (present) (I, you, we, they forms as subject)	▓				

others. Through these occasions I would begin to see the life of the American middle class and the wealth of this consumer society. (Liu Zongren, *Two Years in the Melting Pot.*

2. Women have traditionally entered occupations that are thought to be particularly difficult to organize: jobs in small shops in which women were isolated from other female workers; clerical, secretarial or health-care jobs that replicate the patriarchal family structure; jobs that are seasonal, part-time or temporary. And women themselves have been thought to be particularly difficult to organize. Much of their socialization as females has encouraged them to be passive rather than active. (Ruth Sidel, *Women and Children Last: The Plight of Poor Women in Affluent America.*)

(See Answer Key, p. 160.)

B. Does, Do, *and* Did *in Direct Questions and Negatives*

Questions are signaled by moving an auxiliary verb to the position before the subject and adding a question mark.

She *is working* for a publishing company.
Is she *working* for a publishing company?
Which company *is* she *working* for?

When no auxiliary verb is present (in simple present and simple past tenses), the auxiliaries *does, do,* and *did* are used, always followed by the simple form of the verb.

He *waited* for an hour.
Did he *wait* for an hour?
How long *did* he *wait?*

She *lives* in Los Angeles.
Does she *live* in Los Angeles?
Where *does* she *live?*

Does, do, and *did* are also the auxiliaries used for negation in simple present and simple past tenses.

Interest rates *do* not *change* very often.
The lawyer *did* not *question* the defendant.

In conversation and in informal writing, negative forms are frequently contracted.

They *don't go away* very often.
He *didn't buy* the car.

C. Forms of Be

The forms of the verb *be* are irregular, with the no -*s* form differing from the simple form and with the past tense showing singular and plural forms.

Forms of Be					
Simple	*No -s*	*-s*	*-ing*	*Past*	*Participle*
be	am/are	is	being	was/were	been

Exercise 2

Complete the sentences with the appropriate form of the verb in parentheses.

1. Does your sister (intend) _____ to change her job?
2. Her boss doesn't (pay) _____ her very well.
3. They have never (be) _____ to Paris.
4. This year, my cousin and his wife (be) _____ students at the University of Leningrad.
5. The building was (be) _____ repaired when the gas pipe exploded.

(See Answer Key, p. 160.)

D. Verbs Commonly Confused

Some groups of verbs provide difficulties for language learners. Some examples follow.

rise/raise

Rise is an intransitive verb, irregular in form (rise–rose–risen). It is not followed by an object.

The sun rises at 5:45 tomorrow.

Raise is regular in form; it needs an object.

Linda raised her hand.
The boss raised Malcolm's salary by 5 percent.

lie/lay

Lie is intransitive; that is, it is not followed by an object. It has two different meanings.

lie–lying–lay–lain

He was lying on his bed when I saw him.
She lay down for a nap.

lie–lying–lied–lied

They lied when they were questioned by the police.

Lay is transitive (= *put, set*).
lay–laying–laid–laid

She laid her clothes on the end of the bed.

feel/fall/fill

feel–felt–felt
fall–fell–fallen
fill–filled–filled

She felt sick all day yesterday.
He fell and broke his ankle.
He filled the bottle with water.

rob/steal

rob–robbed–robbed
steal–stole–stolen

He robbed a bank and stole $10,000.
They robbed an old man and stole his watch.

Keep your own lists of examples of other troublesome verbs, such as *make* and *do, borrow* and *lend, say* and *tell.*

E. Coordinate Tags and Question Tags

Coordinate tags and question tags use the auxiliary verb that appears in the independent clause, or they supply *does, do,* or *did* where necessary.

Coordinate tags

She *is* working, and her children *are*, too.
He *lives* in Oklahoma, and so *does* his sister.

Question tags

He *has sent* the receipt, *hasn't* he?
They *signed* the forms, *didn't* they?
They *didn't sign* the forms, *did* they?

Question tags are used more frequently in speech than in writing. Note that when the independent clause is positive, the tag is negative; when the independent clause is negative, the tag is positive.

Exercise 3

Complete the following sentences with the appropriate forms of the verbs.

1. He has been (lie) _____ on his bed for two hours.
2. Ernesto was born and (raise) _____ in Venezuela.
3. When she (fall) _____, she broke her ankle.
4. They studied Spanish, and their parents _____, too.
5. He wants to take the job, _____ he?

(See Answer Key, p. 160.)

Editing Advice

Look at all the complete verbs you have written in your draft, one paragraph at a time. Ask these questions:

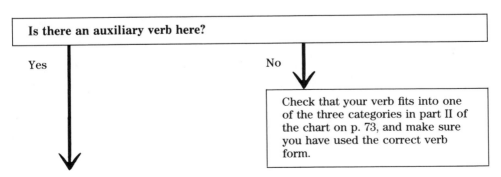

Is there an auxiliary verb here?

Yes

No

Check that your verb fits into one of the three categories in part II of the chart on p. 73, and make sure you have used the correct verb form.

(Flowchart continued)

Troublespot
11

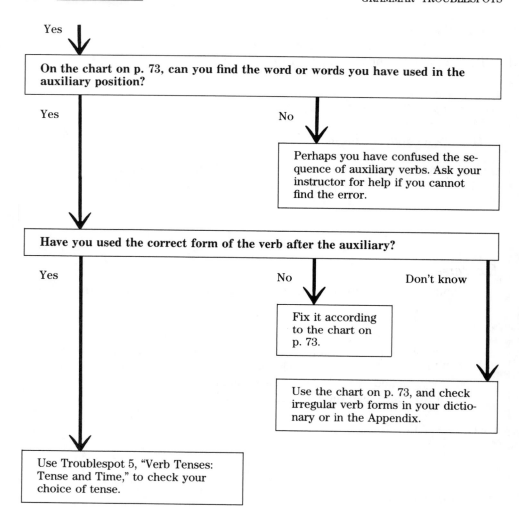

Yes ↓

On the chart on p. 73, can you find the word or words you have used in the auxiliary position?

Yes

No ↓

Perhaps you have confused the sequence of auxiliary verbs. Ask your instructor for help if you cannot find the error.

Have you used the correct form of the verb after the auxiliary?

Yes

No ↓

Don't know

Fix it according to the chart on p. 73.

Use the chart on p. 73, and check irregular verb forms in your dictionary or in the Appendix.

Use Troublespot 5, "Verb Tenses: Tense and Time," to check your choice of tense.

TROUBLESPOT 12

Nouns and Quantity Words

A. *Proper and Common Nouns*

Nouns can be classified as follows:

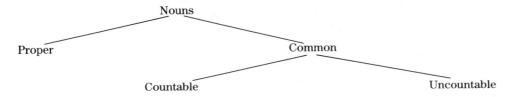

The two major classes are *proper* and *common* nouns.

1. Proper nouns include names of specific people, countries, cities, rivers, languages, places, buildings, schools, months, and days of the week. They begin with a capital letter. (See also items A and D in Troublespot 13, "Articles.")

   My birthday is in *June.*
   The *River Thames* runs through *London,* past the *Houses of Parliament.*
   Henry Wright went to *Columbia University* last *September* to study *French.*

2. If a noun is not a proper noun, it is a common noun. For example, names of objects and animals are common nouns. These nouns do not begin with capital letters. In addition, they are often preceded by one or more *determiners,* as listed.

Articles: *a, an, the* (See Troublespot 13, "Articles.")
Demonstrative adjectives: *this, that, these, those* (See Troublespot 14, "Pronouns and Reference.")

Possessive adjectives: *my, his, our,* etc. (See Troublespot 14, "Pronouns and Reference.")

Possessive nouns: *Sally's, the group's.*

Quantity words: *some, many, much, a lot of,* etc. (See item D.)

Numerals: *one, two, 17,* etc.

B. Countable Nouns

Countable nouns form one of the two classes of common nouns.

1. Countable nouns have a plural form.

The little *girls* sat down on the grass. They ate some *cookies.*

2. The most common way to form a plural of a countable noun is to add *-s* or *-es.* Add it even when there is a numeral included to tell the reader there is more than one. Note that the ending *-y* changes to *-ies* when *-y* is preceded by a consonant.

one girl	two girls
a box	some boxes
one match	a lot of matches
a party	three parties

Some words do not use *-s* for the plural.

one man	two men
a child	many children
that tooth	those teeth

Use your dictionary to check any plurals that you are not sure of.

C. Uncountable Nouns

Uncountable nouns form the second of the two classes of common nouns. In the context of the sentence we used previously, there is an uncountable noun:

The little girls sat down on the *grass.* They ate some cookies.

Grass is here an uncountable, mass noun, meaning *lawn.* (However, in another context, *grass* can be a countable noun, and its plural is *grasses.*)

Countable and uncountable nouns vary from language to language. In English, some nouns do not have a plural form because they are considered essentially uncountable: *advice, enjoyment, equipment, furniture, happiness, homework, information, knowledge, luggage*. (See also Troublespot 13, item A2.)

I asked for some *information*.
He gave me a lot of *information*.
She took a lot of *luggage* on her trip.
She took ten pieces of *luggage* on her trip. (*Luggage* has no plural form; *pieces* indicates the plural.)

There are other mass nouns that can be considered as countable or uncountable, depending on the context:

UNCOUNTABLE *Chocolate* is fattening. (all chocolate: mass noun)
COUNTABLE   He ate a *chocolate*. (one piece, one serving in a box of chocolates: countable)
             Then he ate four more *chocolates*.

D. Quantity Words

Note the use of quantity words with nouns. Some quantity words can be used only with uncountable nouns, with countable singular nouns, or with countable plural nouns. Others can be used with both uncountable nouns and countable plural nouns. Refer to the box "Quantity Words" to check your usage.

Pay special attention to the following:

1. the use of *a few* and *few*, *little* and *a little*

QUANTITY WORDS

With countable singular nouns (girl, child, fact)	With countable plural nouns (girls, children, facts)	With uncountable nouns (luggage, information, happiness)
each every another	several (not) many a few (very) few fewer	a great deal of (not) much a little (very) little less
	With countable plural nouns and with uncountable nouns	
	some no any not any a lot of other lots of	

She has *few* friends.
She has *a few* friends.

These two sentences have different meanings. The former has negative connotations, with *few* the equivalent of *hardly any, almost none,* while the latter tells us that she has some friends. The sentences could be continued as follows:

She has few friends, so she stays home most weekends.
She has a few friends, so she often goes out with them on weekends.

    2. the use of *no* and *not any*

He has *no* friends.
He *doesn't have any* friends.

    In standard English, only one negative expression is used.

NOT *He doesn't have no friends.

Exercise 1

Identify the nouns in the following sentences from *Growing Up* by Russell Baker, and categorize them as common *(C)* or proper *(P);* if common, as countable *(count)* or uncountable *(unc);* and if countable, as singular *(s)* or plural *(pl).* Write down each noun and its identifying abbreviation.

Example:
James bought a dozen eggs, some rice, and a melon.
James: P
eggs: C, count, pl
rice: C, unc
melon: C, count, s

1. I was enjoying the luxuries of a rustic nineteenth-century boyhood, but for the women Morrisonville life had few rewards.
2. Both my mother and grandmother kept house very much as women did before the Civil War.
3. They had no electricity, gas, plumbing, or central heating.
4. For baths, laundry, and dishwashing, they hauled buckets of water from a spring at the foot of a hill.
5. They scrubbed floors on hands and knees, thrashed rugs with carpet beaters, killed and plucked their own chickens, baked bread and pastries, [and] patched the family's clothing on treadle-operated sewing machines.

6. By the end of a summer day a Morrisonville woman had toiled like a serf.
7. [The men] scrubbed themselves in enamel basins and, when supper was eaten, climbed up onto Ida Rebecca's porch to watch the night arrive.
8. Presently the women joined them, and the twilight music of Morrisonville began.

(See Answer Key, p. 160.)

Exercise 2

The student who wrote the following paragraph made mistakes with noun capitals and plurals. Can you identify the errors? Be careful: *some, any,* and *a lot of* can be used with uncountable as well as countable nouns, as in *a lot of money* and *a lot of books* (see item D). How would you explain to the student what was wrong and what must be done to correct the errors?

When I saw my two ancient suitcase, I knew it was time to buy some new luggage. I looked in the windows of all the store in the center of the Town. But all I saw was clothing. I tried on three dress but didn't buy any. At last, I saw a wonderful leather bag made in spain, but it was too expensive.

(See Answer Key, p. 161.)

Editing Advice

Look at any noun in your draft that seems problematic, and ask these questions:

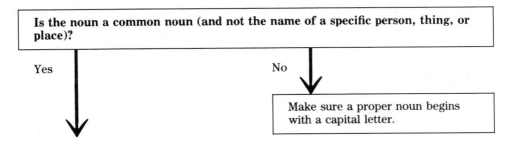

Is the noun a common noun (and not the name of a specific person, thing, or place)?

Yes

No

Make sure a proper noun begins with a capital letter.

(Flowchart continued)

Yes

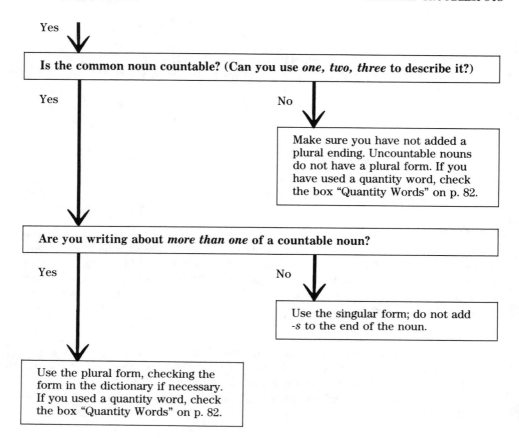

Is the common noun countable? (Can you use *one, two, three* to describe it?)

Yes

No

Make sure you have not added a plural ending. Uncountable nouns do not have a plural form. If you have used a quantity word, check the box "Quantity Words" on p. 82.

Are you writing about *more than one* of a countable noun?

Yes

No

Use the singular form; do not add -*s* to the end of the noun.

Use the plural form, checking the form in the dictionary if necessary. If you used a quantity word, check the box "Quantity Words" on p. 82.

TROUBLESPOT 13

Articles

Other languages do not use articles the way that English does, so some second-language writers find articles to be troublesome. Although there are rules to help you, there are also a lot of exceptions and a lot of fine distinctions to be made. Do not expect to learn a rule, apply it, and then never make another error again. Learning to use articles correctly takes a long time. You need to read a lot, notice how articles are used, and make notes. You should also study and refer to the explanations, examples, and charts in this troublespot.

A. *Type of Noun*

The article you use depends on the noun it modifies, so you must begin by looking at the noun and making the following distinctions (see also Troublespot 12, "Nouns and Quantity Words"):

1. Is it a *common* or a *proper* noun? A proper noun is the name of a specific person, place, or thing (e.g., *James Raimes, Hunter College, England*). All proper nouns begin with a capital letter. Other nouns are common nouns (e.g., *man, school, country*). For the most part, singular proper nouns are not preceded by an article (however, see item D). Plural proper nouns are preceded by *the*, as in *the Great Lakes* and *the Alps*.
2. If the noun is a common noun, is it *countable* or *uncountable* in the sentence in which you want to use it? Here are some examples of countable nouns:

   chair (a chair, two chairs)
   meal (one meal, three meals)
   machine (a machine, some machines)

The following are uncountable, or mass and abstract, nouns:

furniture	information	honesty
rice	gravity	fun
machinery	pollution	vocabulary
equipment	satisfaction	traffic
advice	knowledge	homework

(See also items B and C in Troublespot 12, "Nouns and Quantity Words.")

Difficulty with articles occurs with common nouns because what is considered countable and uncountable varies from language to language. In Spanish, for example, the equivalent of *furniture* is a countable word; in English, *furniture* is always uncountable. It has no plural form, and we cannot say **a furniture*.

Most grammar books list nouns that are regularly uncountable in English. However, someone else's list is never as useful to you as your own. As you continue to read and write in English, keep a list of any uncountable nouns you come across.

B. Specific or Nonspecific Reference

Next decide whether a common noun, in your sentence context, has a specific or a nonspecific reference for the writer and the reader.

1. A *specific* reference is known by the writer and by the reader as something unique, specific, familiar, or previously identified to the reader.

   (a) My daughter is looking after *the dog* this week.

   The writer here expects the reader to know precisely which dog is meant: the family's dog or a dog that the writer has previously identified and perhaps described.

   (b) My neighbor bought *a dog*. My daughter is looking after *the dog* this week.

   Here the dog is identified as the specific dog that the neighbor bought.

   (c) *The dogs* that belong to the night guard have been trained to attack.

   The reader knows specifically which dogs: the ones that belong to the night guard.

2. A *nonspecific* reference is not identified by the writer and by the reader as something known, unique, or familiar.

(a) My daughter is looking after *a dog* this week.

Here the writer does not expect the reader to know the dog in question. It could be any dog—a neighbor's dog, a schoolmate's dog, a poodle, a spaniel, or a sheepdog.

(b) *Dogs* are friendly animals.

Here the writer is making a generalization about all dogs everywhere.

(c) *Some dogs* can be trained to be attack dogs.

Here the writer is not making a generalization about all dogs but is limiting the statement with a quantity word.

C. General Rules for Articles

Once you have made these distinctions about the noun in the context of the meaning of your sentence, you can apply some general rules about article use. But beware! Article use is complex. The accompanying table offers only general guidelines to help you decide which articles to use with common nouns. There

Articles with Common Nouns

		Reference for writer and reader
Type of noun	Specific	Nonspecific
Countable singular	the	a/an
Countable plural	the	Quantity words (*some, a few, many,* etc.). See p. 82 in Troublespot 12, "Nouns and Quantity Words." OR No article with a generalization.
Uncountable	the	Quantity words (*some, a little,* etc.). See p. 82 in Troublespot 12, "Nouns and Quantity Words." OR No article with a generalization.

are many cases that you just have to learn one by one. So whenever you find an exception to a rule, write it down.

Note: There are three important points to remember as you work with the table:

1. A countable singular noun must have an article *(a/an* or *the)* or some other determiner *(this, her, every)* in front of it. A countable singular noun *never stands alone;* for example, in a sentence, *book* by itself is not possible. You must write:

   a book
   the book
   this/that book
   my/his/etc. book
   every/each book

2. Uncountable nouns or countable plural nouns are *never* used with *a/an.* Therefore, forms such as **a furniture, *an advice,* and **a cars* are not possible. (Expressions such as *a few, a little,* and *a lot of* can, however, occur with these nouns.) To express the concept of amounts of uncountable nouns, we have to use expressions such as *two pieces of furniture, several types of food, three teaspoons of sugar, some items of information,* or *a piece of equipment.* (See also Troublespot 12, "Nouns and Quantity Words.")

3. Some nouns can be determined as countable or uncountable only in the context of the sentence in which they are used.

   Life can be hard when you are old. (Here *life* is generic and uncountable; the writer is making a generalization.)

   My grandmother lived *a happy life.* (Here *life* is countable; the writer sees different types of lives: *a happy life, an unhappy life, a useful life,* etc.)

   So what you intend as you write determines the category of countable or uncountable. Only occasionally is it fixed by the word itself.

D. Problematic Terms

The following word groups can cause difficulties.

Unique objects: *the earth, the sun, the moon,* but *Earth*
Places: *France, Central Park, San Francisco, Mount Vesuvius, McDon-*

ald's, but *the United States of America, the United Kingdom, the Sahara,
The Hague, the Statue of Liberty*
Oceans, rivers, seas, and lakes: *the Pacific, the Amazon, the Mediterranean, the Great Lakes,* but *Lake Superior*
Diseases and ailments: *a cold, a headache, the flu,* but *pneumonia, cancer*
Destination: *to go to the store, to go to the post office, to go to the bank, to go to school, to go to church, to go to bed, to go home*
Locations: *at home, in bed, in school, in college*
Expressions of time: *in the morning, in the evening* (but *at night*), *all the time, most of the time* (but *sometimes, in time, on time*)

When trying to decide whether to use an article, ask for help if you need it. Every time you learn a new use of an article, write it down.

Exercise 1

Examine the passage that appears in Troublespot 5, Exercise 1, pp. 35–36. Underline each noun, along with any articles or determiners used (see item A2 in Troublespot 12 for a list of determiners). Try to fit each article or determiner + noun into one of the categories in the table on p. 87. Write down the categories to which you would assign the determiners and nouns:

> Countable or uncountable?
> If countable, singular or plural?
> Specific or nonspecific reference? (Note that demonstratives and possessives always make a specific reference.)

(See Answer Key, p. 161.)

Exercise 2

Read a newspaper article every few days. Underline all the nouns and accompanying articles, and try to explain why you think the writer used the article form that appears. Such frequent close examination of article use will help you understand the relationships between articles and the concepts they express.

Exercise 3

Insert *a/an* or *the* where necessary into the blanks in the following passages. If no article is appropriate, leave the space blank.

1. There is _____ dual labor market—one for men and one
   _(a)

   for _____ women. _____ majority of women are
   _(c) _(d)

   clustered in 20 of _____ 420 occupations listed by
   _(e)

   _____ Bureau of Labor Statistics. (Ruth Sidel, *Women and*
   _(e)

   Children Last: The Plight of Poor Women in Affluent America.)

2. Mrs. Bridge, emptying wastebaskets, discovered _____
   _(a)

   dirty comb in Ruth's basket.

   "What's this doing here?" Ruth inquired late that afternoon

   when she got home and found _____ comb on her dresser.
   _(b)

   "I found it in _____ wastebasket. What was it doing
   _(c)

   there?"

   Ruth said she had thrown it away.

   "Do you think we're made of _____ money?" Mrs.
   _(d)

   Bridge demanded. "When _____ comb gets dirty you don't
   _(e)

   throw it away, you wash it, young lady."

   "It cost _____ nickel," Ruth said angrily. She flung her
   _(f)

   books onto _____ bed and stripped off her sweater.
   _(g)

   "_____ nickels don't grow on _____ trees,"
   _(h) _(i)

   replied Mrs. Bridge, irritated by her manner. (Evan S. Connell, *Mrs.*

   Bridge.)

(See Answer Key, p. 162.)

Editing Advice

If you have problems deciding on *a/an, the,* or no article at all, look at each troublesome noun phrase and ask the following questions:

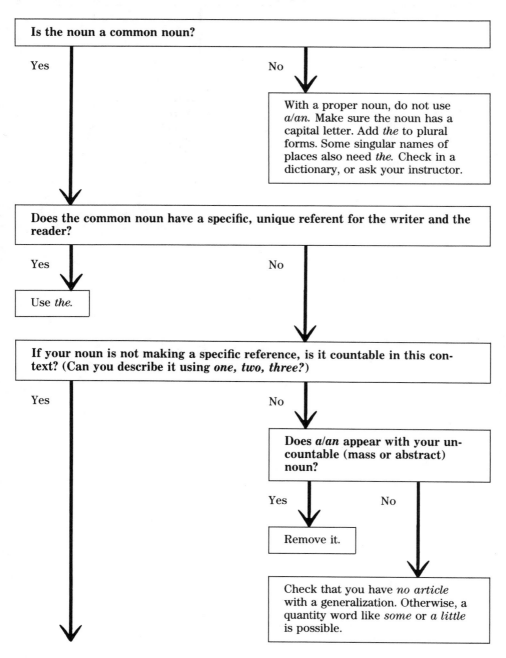

Is the noun a common noun?

Yes

No

With a proper noun, do not use *a/an.* Make sure the noun has a capital letter. Add *the* to plural forms. Some singular names of places also need *the.* Check in a dictionary, or ask your instructor.

Does the common noun have a specific, unique referent for the writer and the reader?

Yes

No

Use *the.*

If your noun is not making a specific reference, is it countable in this context? (Can you describe it using *one, two, three?*)

Yes

No

Does *a/an* appear with your uncountable (mass or abstract) noun?

Yes

No

Remove it.

Check that you have *no article* with a generalization. Otherwise, a quantity word like *some* or *a little* is possible.

(Flowchart continued)

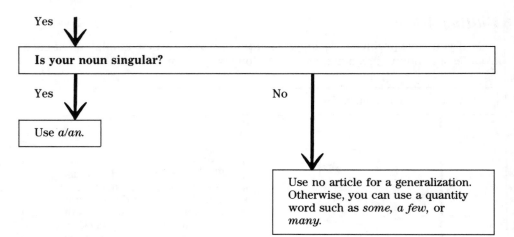

Yes ↓

Is your noun singular?

Yes ↓   No

Use *a/an*.

↓

Use no article for a generalization. Otherwise, you can use a quantity word such as *some*, *a few*, or *many*.

TROUBLESPOT 14

Pronouns and Reference

A. *Personal Pronouns*

The forms of pronouns are rule-governed; that is, which form to use is determined by specific rules. The box shows the rule-governed forms of the personal pronouns. No other forms are possible.

Note the following problem areas:

1. In English, a pronoun agrees in gender (male, female, or neuter) with the noun it refers to (its referent) and not with the noun following it.

   My father never visits his aunt.
   My mother often visits her uncle.

2. Subject and object pronouns are sometimes misused, especially with compound subjects.

PERSONAL PRONOUNS				
Subject pronoun	**Object pronoun**	**Possessive adjective (+ noun)**	**Possessive pronoun**	**Reflexive pronoun**
I	me	my	mine	myself
we	us	our	ours	ourselves
you	you	your	yours	yourself, yourselves
he	him	his	his	himself
she	her	her	hers	herself
it	it	its	—	itself
they	them	their	theirs	themselves
one	one	one's	—	oneself

NOT *Me and Susan want to go shopping.
BUT Susan and I want to go shopping.
NOT *He offered my sister and I a good deal.
BUT He offered my sister and me a good deal.

Every time you write a pronoun as part of a compound subject or object, check the form by removing the other part. You would be left with something that is clearly ungrammatical:

*Me want to go shopping.
*He offered I a good deal.

3. Possessive pronouns stand alone. Possessive adjectives occur before a noun.

That is her coat.
That coat is hers.

4. The forms *its* and *it's* are often confused. *Its* is a possessive adjective, but unlike possessive noun forms, adjectives do not use an apostrophe. *It's* is the contracted form of *it is* or *it has*.

The car is losing *its* muffler. *It's* a new one, too. *It's* been replaced before.

B. Demonstratives

Demonstrative pronouns or adjectives are used to point out (or "demonstrate") what you are referring to.

Demonstrative Adjectives or Pronouns	
Singular	**Plural**
this	these
that	those

Exercise 1

Look at the following passages, and answer the question that follows each.

1. If someone wore shoes with run-over heels, or shoes that had not been shined for a long time, or shoes with broken laces, you could be pretty sure *this* person would be slovenly in other things as well. (Evan S. Connell, *Mrs. Bridge.*)

   What person is the writer referring to?

2. Right now, women still hold only 6 percent of middle-management positions and one percent of jobs in upper management. But *this* will change, says one female executive. (Mary Schnack, "Are Women Bosses Better?")

   What does *this* refer to?

(See Answer Key, p. 162.)

C. Pronoun Reference

When a pronoun is used in a piece of writing, it should be clear to the reader what that pronoun is referring to. The referent should be close by, in the same sentence or one immediately before, and there should be no ambiguity. Here is a problematic use of pronouns:

*When a person has a lot of children, they often can't afford everything.

The sentence is confusing at first because the writer intended *they* to refer to *a person*, but *person* is a singular word. The only plural word for *they* to refer to is *children*. The writer's meaning gets confused. The sentence needs to be revised:

When there are a lot of children in a family, the parents often can't afford everything.

Look at the following sentences:

Sam arrived before my brother did. He had said that he was going to be late.

It is not clear whether *he* refers to *Sam* or *my brother.*

Pay special attention to *it, that, this,* and *they* to make sure that a reader will easily be able to determine what the referent is.

Exercise 2

In the following sentences written by students, circle any personal pronouns, demonstratives, or possessive adjectives that you find. Then decide which word in the passage each pronoun or adjective refers to. Draw a line connecting the pronoun to its referent—the word or words to which it refers.

1. Parents who have to stay in jobs that they don't like in order to support their children often do not spend much time with them.

2. One of our major problems is pollution. Many people are concerned about this, but they cannot find an easy solution.

3. The company hired a new manager. He was only 38 years old, but everybody respected him.

4. The father and his son used to ride their bicycles to work.

5. Children love their toys. They usually have one favorite, which they take to bed with them.

(See Answer Key, p. 162.)

D. Avoiding Errors

Remember the following points about pronouns and pronoun reference:

1. A pronoun is not used to restate a long subject.

NOT *My brother who works for a bank on Long Island he visits our country every year.
BUT My brother who works for a bank on Long Island visits our country every year.

2. Singular words need singular pronouns.

a person: he or she
everyone, everybody, someone: he or she
each, every + noun: he, she, it
news: it
information: it
happiness: it

3. A pronoun should have a clear referent, close enough to it in the piece of writing to avoid ambiguity.

Editing Advice

Look at each problematic pronoun in your piece of writing, and ask these questions:

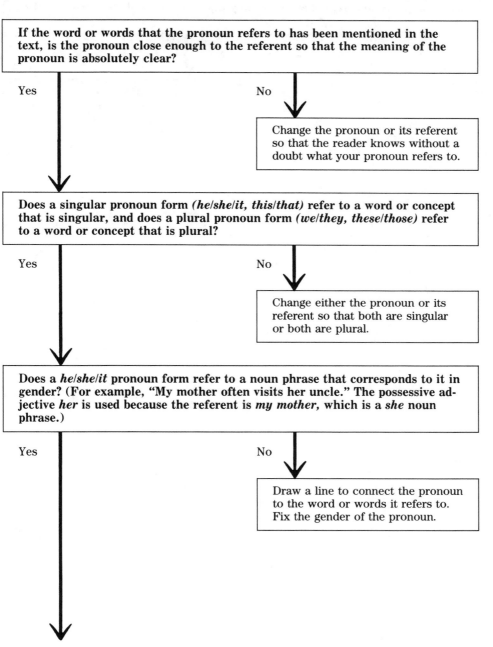

If the word or words that the pronoun refers to has been mentioned in the text, is the pronoun close enough to the referent so that the meaning of the pronoun is absolutely clear?

Yes

No

Change the pronoun or its referent so that the reader knows without a doubt what your pronoun refers to.

Does a singular pronoun form *(he/she/it, this/that)* refer to a word or concept that is singular, and does a plural pronoun form *(we/they, these/those)* refer to a word or concept that is plural?

Yes

No

Change either the pronoun or its referent so that both are singular or both are plural.

Does a *he/she/it* pronoun form refer to a noun phrase that corresponds to it in gender? (For example, "My mother often visits her uncle." The possessive adjective *her* is used because the referent is *my mother,* which is a *she* noun phrase.)

Yes

No

Draw a line to connect the pronoun to the word or words it refers to. Fix the gender of the pronoun.

(Flowchart continued)

Yes

Is the pronoun form you have used exactly the same form as one shown in the boxes on pp. 93 and 94? (Check especially that you have not confused *its* with *it's*.)

No

Ask for help if you need it.

TROUBLESPOT 15

Adjectives and Adverbs

A. Uses of Adjectives and Adverbs

Adjectives give information about nouns and noun phrases and answer the question "What kind?"; adverbs give information about verbs and verb phrases or about adjectives and answer the question "How?"

Adjective
I like a quiet room. / I like quiet rooms.
The room was very quiet.

Adverb
She speaks quietly.
He is quietly efficient.

B. Features of Adjectives and Adverbs

Note the following features of adjectives and adverbs.

1. Adjectives have no plural form.

   A different story
   Some different stories

2. Adjectives expressing nationality always have a capital letter.

   A Chinese restaurant
   A French meal

3. Adverbs frequently end in *-ly*.

   quickly
   happily
   efficiently

C. Forms to Learn

1. Although *-ly* is usually an adverb ending, some adjectives end in *-ly.*

   friendly
   lively
   lovely

   Use "in a _____ way" with these adjectives to explain how an action was performed.

   She spoke to me in a friendly way.

2. Some adverb forms do not use a *-ly* ending.

Adjective	*Adverb*
hard	hard
fast	fast

3. Note the spelling of the adverb when an adjective ends in a vowel + *l.*

careful	carefully
successful	successfully

4. Take care with *hard* and *hardly. Hardly* has a negative connotation.

   He hardly ever offers to help.
   I'd hardly describe her looks as beautiful!

D. Position of Adjectives in a Series

Adjectives in a series tend to occur in a certain order, though there are frequent exceptions.

Usual Order of Adjectives

Determiner	Opinion	Physical description				Nationality	Religion	Material	Noun	Head noun
		Size	Shape	Age	Color					
three	beautiful			old						houses
my			long		blue			silk	evening	gown
a	delicious					French				meal
her		big		old		English		oak	writing	desk
Lee's	charming						Catholic			teacher
several		little	round					marble	coffee	tables

Exercise 1

Look carefully at each of the following noun phrases, and determine which one of the categories in the chart each word belongs to.

1. that sophisticated young Italian model
2. his comfortable white velvet couch
3. two middle-aged Catholic bishops
4. their charming little wood cabin

(See Answer Key, p. 163.)

E. Adjectives and Prepositions

Some adjectives used after a verb phrase (predicate adjectives) are regularly used with prepositions.

I am afraid of ghosts.
I confess that I am proud of winning the race.

Whenever you come across this adjective + preposition structure in your reading, write down the whole sentence in which it appears. Here are some to start off your list:

aware of	satisfied with	full of
suspicious of	happy about	proud of
afraid of	interested in	jealous of
fond of	different from	

(See also Troublespot 17, "Prepositions and Phrasal Verbs.")

F. Comparisons

We add endings to short adjectives to form comparatives or superlatives, but for long adjectives and for *-ly* adverbs, we use *more* and *most* for the comparative and superlative forms.

cool	cooler (than)	the coolest
intelligent	more intelligent	the most intelligent
carefully	more carefully	the most carefully

Sally is smart and witty. She is *smarter* and *wittier* than her sister.
She was *the smartest* in her class, but not *the wittiest.*
She was *more serious* about her work than other students, and she was the *most ambitious* student in her class.
She works *more efficiently* than her classmates.

G. Position of Adverbs

Adverbs can appear in different positions in a sentence.

Usual Order of Adverbs

Adverb	Subject	Adverb	Verb + Object	Adverb
Systematically,	the teacher		reviewed the tenses.	
	The teacher		reviewed the tenses	systematically.
	The teacher	systematically	reviewed the tenses.	

Although an adverb can move around in a sentence, it can *never* be placed between the verb and a short object. The following sentence is not possible in English:

*The teacher reviewed *systematically* the tenses.

Another type of adverb that can move around in the sentence is one that tells about the whole sentence: adverbs like *fortunately, actually, obviously, certainly,* and *recently.*

Certainly, he is very intelligent.
He is *certainly* very intelligent.
He is very intelligent, *certainly.*

The adverb *only* also has the ability to move around in the sentence, but its position changes the meaning of the sentence. In the following sentence, the

word *only* can be inserted at each one of the points indicated, and only numbers 4 and 6 have the same meaning.
(The scene is a bus that has been involved in an accident.)

	The	passenger	hurt	his	arm	
1	2		3	4	5	6

H. Adverbs of Frequency

Many adverbs of frequency tell about the whole sentence and not just about the verb; they do not always end in *-ly*, and they can be used in different positions in the sentence. Some of these adverbs are *always, sometimes, often, seldom, usually,* and *frequently.*

He is *always* tactful. (after a single *be* verb)
He *always* behaves tactfully. (before a single verb)
He has *always* spoken tactfully to his boss. (after the first auxiliary verb)

I. Compound Adjectives

Note that compound adjectives use hyphens and a singular form.

Her son is six years old.
She has a six-year-old son.

Compound adjectives of physical description use the *-ed* form.

left-handed   bow-legged
broad-shouldered   dark-haired
flat-chested

Exercise 2

Write a story beginning with the sentence "As I was walking to the bus stop in the rain, I saw Helen. She was with Alfred." In it, use adjectives and adverbs that have real significance for your story. If you are working in a computer lab with other students, write only one paragraph at a time. Then move to somebody else's computer and continue that person's story.

Editing Advice

Read through your essay. If you need to check your use of an adjective or adverb at any point, stop and ask yourself these questions:

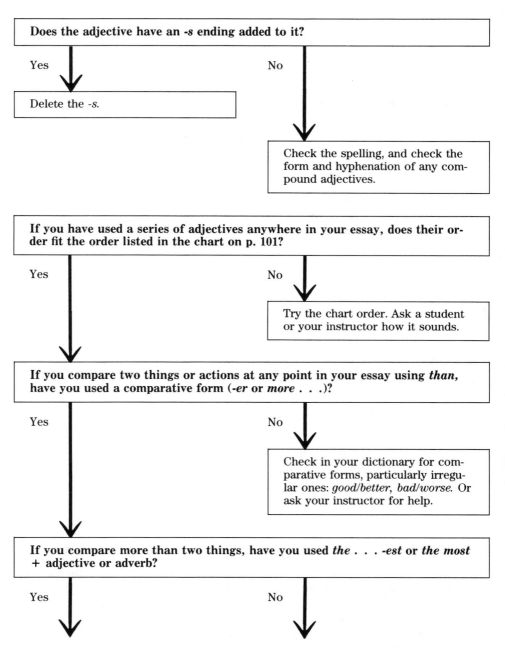

Does the adjective have an *-s* ending added to it?

Yes

No

Delete the *-s*.

Check the spelling, and check the form and hyphenation of any compound adjectives.

If you have used a series of adjectives anywhere in your essay, does their order fit the order listed in the chart on p. 101?

Yes

No

Try the chart order. Ask a student or your instructor how it sounds.

If you compare two things or actions at any point in your essay using *than,* have you used a comparative form (*-er* or *more . . .*)?

Yes

No

Check in your dictionary for comparative forms, particularly irregular ones: *good/better, bad/worse.* Or ask your instructor for help.

If you compare more than two things, have you used *the . . . -est* or *the most* + adjective or adverb?

Yes

No

(Flowchart continued)

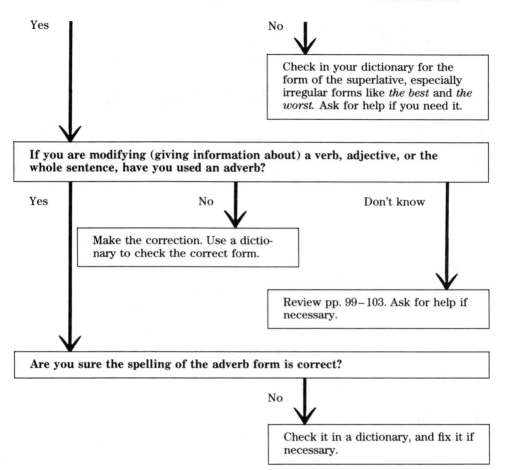

Yes | No

Check in your dictionary for the form of the superlative, especially irregular forms like *the best* and *the worst*. Ask for help if you need it.

If you are modifying (giving information about) a verb, adjective, or the whole sentence, have you used an adverb?

Yes | No | Don't know

Make the correction. Use a dictionary to check the correct form.

Review pp. 99–103. Ask for help if necessary.

Are you sure the spelling of the adverb form is correct?

No

Check it in a dictionary, and fix it if necessary.

TROUBLESPOT 16

Infinitive, -ing, and Participle Forms

A. Forms of the Verb

In addition to present and past tense forms, verbs have an infinitive form, an *-ing* form, and a participle *(-ed/-en)* form. Their uses can be confusing. Note the forms involved.

Infinitive	*-ing*	*Participle*
to surprise	surprising	surprised
to take	taking	taken

See also Troublespot 11, item A.

B. Uses of the Infinitive

The infinitive (*to* + simple form of the verb) is used in the following ways:

1. After a verb

   Verbs such as *want, promise, hope, pretend, plan, manage, need, expect, forget, decide, choose,* and *prove* are followed immediately by an infinitive.

   They expect to win the game.
   She needs to apply for a scholarship.
   The negotiations will probably prove to have a happy ending.

2. After verb and object

   With verbs that take an object, such as *force, allow, expect, believe, want, need, persuade,* and *urge,* the infinitive follows the object.

She persuaded us to wait.
She urged her supporters not to leave.

3. After certain adjectives and nouns

Adjectives such as *anxious, eager, sorry, proud, easy, difficult, right,* and *wrong* can be followed by infinitives.

It is easy (for you) to get to my house.
He was eager to meet his new boss.

Some nouns (such as *way, place, time, decision, job,* and *aim*) are frequently followed by an infinitive.

He has no place to relax.
It is time to go.
Her decision to leave the country was made very quickly.

4. To express purpose

He is working at night (in order) to earn more money.

C. *The Infinitive Without* to

The infinitive form without *to* is used in the following idiomatic expressions.

1. After the causative *make, let, have* + object

He made his sister drive the whole way.
He had her pay for the gas, too.
She let her boyfriend borrow her computer.

2. After the verb *help*

They helped us solve the problem.

D. *Uses of* -ing *Forms*

-ing words are used in the following ways:

1. As part of a complete active verb phrase, with auxiliaries

He is painting the house.
He has been painting the house all day.

2. To include additional information in the sentence (but avoid dangling modifiers!)

The man wearing blue jeans is her brother.
I saw him hurrying along the street.
Driving over the bridge, we admired the lights of the city.

But you cannot write

*Driving over the bridge, the lights looked magnificent.

Why not? Because the lights weren't driving. This is an example of a dangling modifier. An initial -*ing* modifier must give information about the subject of the sentence. Revise the sentence like this:

Driving over the bridge, we all thought the lights looked magnificent.

Note: -ing phrases always express an active meaning.

3. As adjectives

a crying baby
an interesting movie
The play was very boring.

4. As nouns *(-ing* nouns are called *gerunds)*
   a. As the subject of the sentence

Swimming is good for you.

Note that an -*ing* subject is followed by a third-person singular *(he/she/ it)* verb.

Driving on icy roads *makes* me feel nervous.

b. As the object of certain verbs

She dislikes swimming.
He enjoys playing tennis.
She avoids driving on icy roads.
She finished cooking dinner at 8 P.M.
Can you imagine not wanting to go on vacation?
She stopped smoking recently.
They ended up lending us everything.

There are other verbs regularly followed by the -*ing* noun form. Note them as you come across them in your reading.

c. After certain verb phrases with prepositions

They *insisted on paying* for themselves.

Other common verb + preposition phrases include these:

approve of	get (be) used to
blame for	look forward to
complain about	suspect of
get (be) accustomed to	thank for

(See also Troublespot 17, "Prepositions and Phrasal Verbs," items F and H.)

5. In idiomatic expressions with the verb *go*

> to go shopping
> > fishing
> > dancing
> > bowling
> > skating
> > swimming
> > sightseeing

6. In other idiomatic expressions

After *worth:*

It's not worth waiting for so long.

After *difficulty:*

They had difficulty finding the right room.
BUT It was difficult for them to find the right room.

After *have fun, have a good time:*

They had fun watching the game.

After *spend time:*

I spent a lot of time doing my homework.

E. Common Verbs with Infinitive and/or -ing

Some verbs can only be followed by an infinitive form, and some only by an *-ing* form. Other verbs can be followed by either one, sometimes with a slight difference in meaning. Consult a dictionary or ask your instructor.

Verb with infinitive (to + simple form)	Verb with -ing	Verb with either infinitive or -ing
want	enjoy	try
decide	avoid	hate
hope	dislike	like
need	imagine	remember
choose	finish	begin
expect	deny	continue

Add to this list.

Sensory verbs like *see*, *hear*, and *watch* are followed by the *-ing* form if the activity is in progress and only part of it is witnessed and by the infinitive form without *to* if the event is witnessed in its entirety.

I heard her playing the piano as I walked past.
I heard Brendel play a Schubert sonata at the concert last night.

Exercise 1

Fill in a correct form of the given verb in each sentence (the infinitive with or without *to* or the *-ing* form).

1. They want (arrange) _____ all the details carefully.
2. You can't expect your boss (wait) _____ for you all day.
3. They really enjoy (have) _____ nothing to do.
4. He hasn't finished (write) _____ his essay yet.
5. She complained about (be) _____ the only person without the books.
6. They forced the hostages (lie) _____ on the floor.
7. Then they made them (close) _____ their eyes.
8. Sometimes we tell a lie (prevent) _____ embarrassment.
9. Is it difficult (make) _____ an omelette?
10. When did you last go (skate)_____?

(See Answer Key, p. 163.)

F. Uses of Participle (-ed/-en) Forms

Participles are used in the following ways:

1. As part of a complete active verb phrase, with *have* auxiliaries

   He has painted the house.
   They had painted the house before I arrived.

2. As part of a complete passive verb phrase with *be/being* auxiliaries

   The house is being painted.
   The house might have been painted.

   (See also Troublespot 9, "Active and Passive.")

3. To add information to a sentence

   Confused by the people and traffic, Jack wandered around for hours before he found his sister's apartment building.
   Begun five years ago, the building had never progressed beyond the foundations.
   The food prepared in that restaurant is very exotic.

   Note that all the participial phrases in items 2 and 3 express a passive meaning.

4. As adjectives

   The exhausted swimmer collapsed after the race.
   The swimmer felt exhausted.

G. Confusion of -ing and Participle Forms

Sometimes writers mix up the *-ing* and the participle *(-ed/-en)* forms of transitive verbs. Study these correct sentences:

The movie amused the audience. (*Amuse* is a transitive verb.)
The movie was (very) amusing. (active meaning)
The audience was (very) amused. (Passive meaning. The audience was amused *by* the movie.)

Exercise 2

Write as many sentences as you can using each of the following groups of words. Use the past tense verb form, the *-ing* form, and the participle *(-ed/-en)* forms of the first word of each group. Add any other words you need.

1.   annoy   Sarah   the loud radio

2.   confuse   the students   the difficult lecture

3.   surprise   we/us   the end of the movie

(See Answer Key, p. 164.)

Exercise 3

In the following passages, fill in the infinitive form with or without *to*, the *-ing* form, or the participle form of the given verb.

1. When I watch Emily (collect) _____ eggs in the evening,
   (a)

   (fish) _____ with Jim on the river or (enjoy)
   (b)

   _____ an old-fashioned picnic in the orchard with the en-
   (c)

   tire family, I know we've (find) _____ just what we were
   (d)

   (look) _____ for. (From Jim Doherty, "Mr. Doherty Builds
   (e)

   His Dream Life."

2. I expected . . . that I would have difficulty personally (adjust)

   _____ to (do) _____ housework. This expecta-
   (a)   (b)

   tion was all the greater because I came from a home in which my

   father never did any housework, and I had never (be)

   _____ (oblige) _____ (do) _____ any
   (c)   (d)   (e)

   either. . . . A few things about child care are unpleasant, such as

   (have) _____ to wake up at five in the morning when a
   (f)

little girl wants (play) _____ or (take) _____

 (g) (h)

care of a baby who can only cry because she can't tell you that her

head hurts or she has a fever. (William R. Beer, *Househusbands.*)

3. Man has always shown a great capacity for (adjust) _____

 (a)

to change. Past generations have survived floods and ice ages, fam-

ines and world wars. But when (deal) _____ with the envi-

 (b)

ronment, there is a grave danger in (rely) _____ on adapta-

 (c)

tion alone: societies could end up (wait) _____ too long.

 (d)

Many of the global processes under way, like the wholesale destruc-

tion of species, are irreversible. Others, like global climate changes

(cause) _____ by man, are so profound that if (allow)

 (e)

_____ (progress) _____ too far, they could prove

 (f) (g)

(be) _____ overwhelming. (Philip Elmer-DeWitt, "Preparing

 (h)

for the Worst.")

(See Answer Key, p. 164.)

Exercise 4

Rewrite the following pairs of sentences as one sentence by using -*ing* or a participle phrase to incorporate the first sentence into the second. Make the second sentence your new independent clause.

Example:

He felt hungry.
He bought three slices of pizza.
Feeling very hungry, he bought three slices of pizza.

1. She wanted to get the job.
   She arrived early for the interview.

2. The gray-haired woman is wearing a blue coat.
   The gray-haired woman is my mother.
3. The movie excited us.
   We saw a movie last week.
4. The student was confused by the examination questions.
   The student failed the exam.
5. A painting was stolen from the museum yesterday.
   The painting was extremely valuable.

(See Answer Key, p. 164.)

Editing Advice

If you have problems with infinitives, *-ing* forms, or participle forms, ask the following questions about each troublesome sentence:

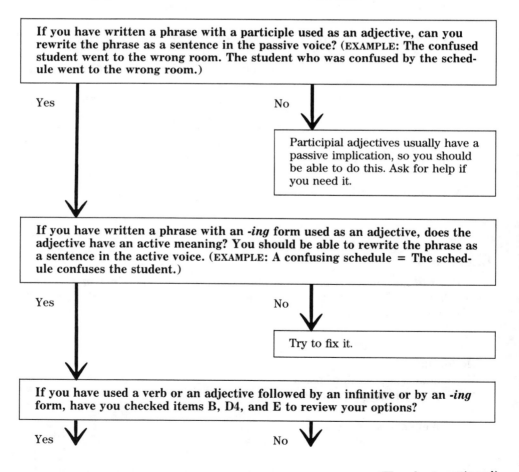

(Flowchart continued)

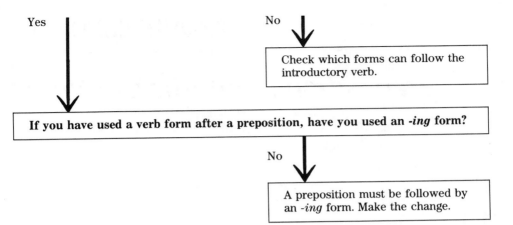

Yes

No

Check which forms can follow the
introductory verb.

If you have used a verb form after a preposition, have you used an *-ing* form?

No

A preposition must be followed by
an *-ing* form. Make the change.

Prepositions and Phrasal Verbs

A. Prepositions

Prepositions are difficult words for language learners since they do not appear to operate according to clear sets of rules. They are often idiomatic and call for one-by-one learning. Each time you come across a preposition, note its use and its meaning.

These are some features of prepositions:

1. They are followed by noun phrases.
2. They are frequently combined with verbs or adjectives to form idiomatic expressions.
3. They are often used to form phrasal verbs. Such verbs are found in only a few languages (German, Dutch, and Swedish, for example), so they are difficult for speakers of other languages.

Examples of these features will appear in this troublespot.

B. Prepositions of Place

The pictures on the following page illustrate prepositions. The first set of pictures shows how some prepositions of place are used.

The second set of pictures illustrates the difference between *in front of* and *in the front of* and *in back of* and *in the back of*:

The truck is in front of the car.
The car is in back of the truck.

The man is in the front of the car.
The dog is in the back of the car.

on the table   at the table   under the table   above the table

in the drawer   on the floor   next to the table

by the window   over the table   in the corner   on the wall

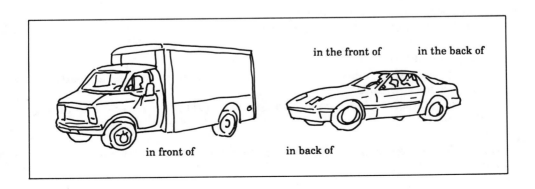

in the front of   in the back of

in front of   in back of

Note the following uses of prepositions of place:

at home, at school, at work, at the top of the page, at a party, at the bottom of the stairs

in bed, in jail, in a picture, in a mirror, in the corner (of a room), in one's hand, in the water, in the river, in the newspaper, in the drawer, in the front row, in a car, in a taxi

on the left, on the right, on the corner (of a street), on the shelf, on the fifth floor, on a farm, on a bicycle, on a train, on top of (the cabinet, the car)

C. Prepositions of Direction

The following show opposing directions:

into	-	out of (get into and out of a car or a taxi)
on (to)	-	off (get on and off a bus)
toward	-	away from
to	-	from
over	-	under

D. Prepositions of Time

The prepositions *at, on,* and *in* are frequently confused. Note how they are used to show increasingly general times:

at: with times of the day
on: with dates and days of the week
in: with years, months, and seasons

He got up at 6 o'clock.
John Fitzgerald Kennedy, president of the United States, was assassinated on November 22, 1963.
Madame Curie won her second Nobel Prize in 1911 for her work with radioactivity.

Note: on the weekend, in the morning, in the afternoon, in the evening, at night.

E. Tricky Prepositions

since/for

> *Since* indicates a point in time. *For* indicates the length of a period of time.

I have lived in St. Louis for ten years.
I have lived in St. Louis since 1982.

during/for

> *For* indicates the length of a period of time. *During* indicates the time period surrounding an event.

He is away for the afternoon.
I'll call him during the evening.

near/next to

> *Near* indicates general proximity. *Next to* indicates more direct proximity.

They live near each other (a few blocks apart).
His house is next to mine (they are adjoining houses).

between/among

> *Between* indicates a position relative to two markers. *Among* indicates a position relative to more than two.

The file is between the computer and the fax machine.
The document is among my papers somewhere.

by/until

> *By* indicates a point in time, a deadline; it is the equivalent of *no later than*. *Until* indicates length of time.

We have to register by August 28.
It's only June. We don't have to register until August.
They waited until August 27 to register for their courses.
She was reading until midnight.
She had finished her assignments by midnight, so she called her parents then.

because/because of

> *Because* is a conjunction followed by a subject and verb (S + V) to form a dependent clause. *Because of* is followed by a noun phrase.

The Wimbledon tennis matches were delayed because it was raining.
The Wimbledon tennis matches were delayed because of bad weather.

F. Verb + Preposition

Certain verbs are frequently found with specific prepositions. These are some common combinations:

rely on
depend on
insist on
concentrate on
congratulate someone on something
consist of
take care of
apologize to someone for something
blame someone for something
thank someone for something
complain about
worry about
smile at
arrive in (a country or city)
arrive at (a building, landmark, or event)
explain something to someone
explain to someone that (what, why) . . .

G. Adjective + Preposition

In addition, some adjectives are often accompanied by prepositions to form idiomatic expressions:

aware of
proud of
tired of
jealous of
afraid of
ashamed of
interested in
responsible for
anxious about
sorry for/about
happy for/about/with
content with
angry with/at/for/about
grateful to/for

H. Prepositions + -ing

Prepositions are followed by noun phrases, so a preposition will be followed by the *-ing* form (the gerund), which is a noun form.

I thanked him for helping me.
They blamed the bad weather for causing the accident.
He is good at solving mathematical problems.
She swam a mile without stopping.

Confusion occurs when the preposition *to* is used, since frequently *to* is part of an infinitive and precedes the simple form of the verb. *To* is a preposition in the following phrases:

look forward to
get (be) used to
get (be) accustomed to

I am looking forward to seeing my family again.
She is getting used to working longer hours now that she has a full-time job.

Exercise 1

Insert an appropriate preposition in the following sentences.

1. She is living _____ Denver, Colorado.
2. Her parents live _____ the same street.
3. Her brother lives _____ 356 Clinton Street.
4. He knocked the glass _____ the table and it smashed on the tile floor.
5. It often rains _____ the night.
6. It often rains _____ night.
7. He was very proud _____ his son's achievements.
8. Her future plans depend _____ her father's health.
9. His family arrived _____ Seattle last month.
10. This dessert consists _____ cream, gelatine, sugar, and eggs.

(See Answer Key, p. 165.)

I. No Prepositions

The following expressions are highly idiomatic in English and include no prepositions:

to go home
to arrive home
to be/stay home
to go shopping/swimming/skating/bowling

J. Phrasal Verbs

A phrasal verb is a verb + particle. Particles are almost the same as prepositions, but they function in different ways. These are the features of phrasal verbs:

1. A phrasal verb is a verb + particle. This combination takes on an idiomatic meaning.

put off = postpone
put out = extinguish
She put off going to the dentist.
He put out the flames with a glass of water.

2. Some phrasal verbs are used with specific prepositions.

put up with
look down on
check up on
I can't put up with that noise any longer!

3. Some phrasal verbs are separable.

She wanted to know the meaning of a word, so she found a dictionary and looked the word up/looked up the word/looked it up.
He filled the form out/filled out the form.

Exercise 2

Write sentences using the following phrasal verbs. Try to make the meaning of the phrasal verb clear in your sentence. If you need to check the meaning, use a dictionary.

Example:
put on
It was getting cold, so she put her jacket on.

turn up	take after
give up	look after
get up	look for
take off	throw away

Exercise 3

Choose any appropriate word (not necessarily a preposition) that will fit into the blanks.

1. Before she went to bed, she turned _____ the lights.
2. I'll write the report _____ next Tuesday. That's a promise.
3. He is looking forward to _____ his nephew when he visits his sister next week.
4. He didn't turn _____ on time, so the meeting had to be called _____.
5. When my daughter was sick, Nora's sister offered to help look _____ her.
6. They called to congratulate him _____ _____ the prize. (Use *win* as the verb.)
7. They wanted to watch TV, so I turned _____ _____ immediately. (Use the pronoun *it.*)
8. He explained _____ me why I had to stay and work _____ 8 o'clock _____ the evening.
9. He said he thought he could rely _____ me, but then he apologized _____ _____ me to work late two nights in a row.
10. I decided not to complain _____ the boss _____ my long working hours.

(See Answer Key, p. 165.)

Editing Advice

To check your use of prepositions and phrasal verbs, ask the following questions as you read through your piece of writing:

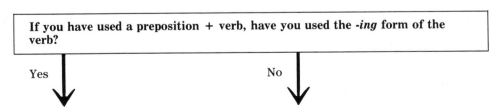

If you have used a preposition + verb, have you used the *-ing* form of the verb?

Yes   No

(Flowchart continued)

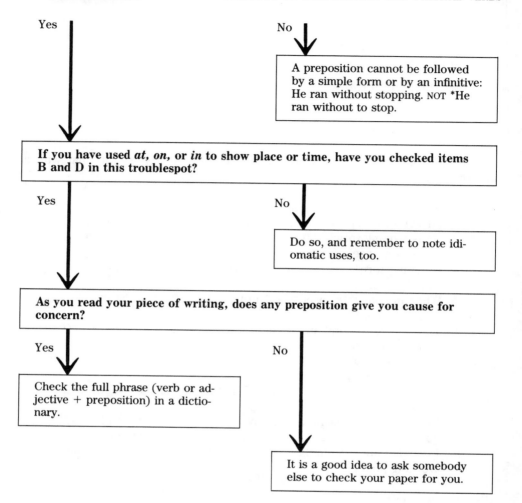

TROUBLESPOT 18

Relative Clauses

A. *Function of Relative Clauses*

A relative clause tells the reader more about a noun phrase.

The boy kept looking at his watch.
[The boy was waiting at the corner.]
The boy *who was waiting at the corner* kept looking at his watch.

The independent clause is *The boy kept looking at his watch.* The relative clause *who was waiting on the corner* tells the reader some necessary information: It tells the reader which boy we mean.

B. *Form of Relative Clauses*

A relative clause is combined with *(embedded in)* an independent clause in the following way, with the relative clause following its referent (the head noun it refers to).

1. The woman is a teacher.
   [The woman lives next door to me.]
   The woman *who lives next door to me* is a teacher.
2. I bought a suit.
   [My mother liked the suit.]
   I bought the suit *that my mother liked.*
   OR I bought the suit *my mother liked.*

   (*That* may be omitted if the relative pronoun is the object of the relative clause; see item F.)

3. The person was wearing the same suit.
   [I took over the person's job.]
   The person *whose job I took over* was wearing the same suit.

Whose and *who's* are pronounced the same way. However, *who's* is a contraction of *who is*.

C. *Relative Pronouns*

Use the following box to help you determine which relative pronoun to use.

Relative Pronouns		
Position within clause	*Relative pronoun referent*	
	PEOPLE	THINGS/CONCEPTS
Subject	who that	which that
Direct object	who/whom that (omitted)	which that (omitted)
Possessive	whose	whose of which

D. *When to Use* That *and When Not to Use* That

In American usage, *that* is usually preferable to *which*. *That* (and not *what*) follows words like *everything* and *something:* Everything that I own is old. In some cases, though, *that* is not used.

1. *That* is not used in nonrestrictive relative clauses. In a nonrestrictive relative clause, the relative clause gives additional information about a unique person, thing, or event. The clause does not define or restrict which person, thing, or event the writer means but rather adds information about a person or thing that has already been identified. Relative clauses like this use *who, whom,* and *which* (but not *that*); they are also separated from the independent clause by commas, as in these sentences:

Douglas, who liked to argue, made his mother annoyed.
Here is my father, whom you met last week in Sacramento.
He sold his Cadillac, which he had bought in 1985.

Note that in each case the referent is unique: Douglas, my father, his Cadillac. If your referent is not a proper noun or a unique person or thing, the relative clause is restrictive, and you will not use commas.

2. *That* is not used when the relative pronoun refers to the whole of the previous clause:

He moved to the country, which (= a thing that) he had always wanted to do.

3. *That* is not used when the relative pronoun follows immediately after a preposition:

The controversy to which the author is referring has not been resolved.
OR The controversy that the author is referring to has not been resolved.

E. Agreement of Verb in a Relative Clause

The relative pronouns *who, which,* and *that* can refer to singular or plural noun phrases. When *who, which,* or *that* is the subject of its relative clause, the verb of that clause agrees with the noun phrase that the pronoun refers to:

The journalist who wants to interview you works for a business magazine.

The journalists who want to interview you work for a business magazine.

Note that we do *not* mention the subject of the sentence again after a relative clause. The following sentence is *wrong* in English:

*The journalists who want to interview you *they* work for a business magazine.

They should be omitted here. The subject of the verb *work*—that is, *journalists*—has already been stated.

F. Omitting the Relative Pronoun

When the relative pronoun—*who(m), which,* or *that*—is the object of its own clause, it may be omitted.

I bought the suit that my mother liked. [My mother liked the suit.]
I bought the suit my mother liked.
I didn't buy the suit (that) I really liked!

G. Prepositions and Relative Clauses

Sentences that use a preposition in a relative clause require special attention.

> The woman is a teacher.
> [My friend is talking to the woman.]

There are five possible ways to combine these sentences:

1. The woman *whom* my friend is talking to is a teacher.
2. The woman *who* my friend is talking to is a teacher. [Some people now accept the *who* form in the object position in the relative clause. Others, however, insist on the first version (with *whom*), which is much more formally "correct." Ask your instructor which form you should use in your classes.]
3. The woman *that* my friend is talking to is a teacher.
4. The woman my friend is talking to is a teacher.
5. The woman to whom my friend is talking is a teacher. (formal usage)

Note that you cannot use *that* as a relative pronoun immediately after a preposition. In the last example, *whom* is the only pronoun possible after *to*.

Exercise 1

Combine the following pairs of sentences into one sentence each, using a relative clause. (Refer to the box in item C if you need help.) Pay special attention to which one of the two sentences you want to embed in the other. How does it change the sense of the sentence if you do it another way? Only one of these sentences will need commas around the relative clause. Which one is it?

1. The man was awarded a prize. The man won the race.
2. The girl is sitting in the front row. The girl asks a lot of questions.
3. The people are from California. I met the people at a party last night.
4. The house is gigantic. He is living in the house.
5. Mrs. McHam lives next door to me. Mrs. McHam is a lawyer.
6. The journalist has won a lot of prizes. You read the journalist's story yesterday.
7. The radio was made in Taiwan. I bought the radio.
8. She told her friends about the book. She had just read the book.
9. The man is a radio announcer. I am looking after the man's dog.

10. The pediatrician lives in my neighborhood. I recommended the pediatrician.

(See Answer Key, p. 165.)

Exercise 2

Identify and correct the errors in the following sentences.

1. Two years ago, my friend Zhi-Wei, who just got married. He worked as a manager in a big company.
2. A boy from high school was the worst person in the class took another's boy's sweater.
3. My sister, whose living in Atlanta, writes to me every week.
4. I have found the book that I was looking for it.
5. The students in my class who studies hard will pass the test.

(See Answer Key, p. 165.)

Exercise 3

Combine the following pairs of sentences by making the second sentence into a relative clause. Separate the clauses with commas because you are providing additional rather than necessary information. Introduce the relative clause with expressions like *some of whom/which, one of whom/which, many of whom/which, none of whom/which, neither of whom/which,* and *most of whom/which.*

Example:

She has three sisters. None of them will help her.
She has three sisters, none of whom will help her.

1. Thirty-three people attended the lecture. Most of them lived in the neighborhood.
2. They waited half an hour for the committee members. Some members just did not show up.
3. I sang three songs. One of them was "Singing in the Rain."
4. The statewide poetry competition was held last month, and she submitted four poems. None of them won a prize.
5. On every wall of his house, he has hundreds of books. Most of them are detective novels.

(See Answer Key, p. 166.)

Editing Advice

If you want to check that you have used a relative clause correctly, ask the following questions:

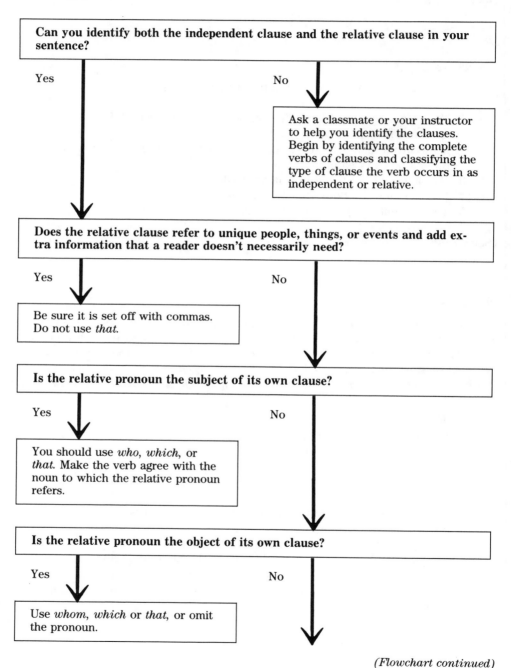

Can you identify both the independent clause and the relative clause in your sentence?

Yes

No

Ask a classmate or your instructor to help you identify the clauses. Begin by identifying the complete verbs of clauses and classifying the type of clause the verb occurs in as independent or relative.

Does the relative clause refer to unique people, things, or events and add extra information that a reader doesn't necessarily need?

Yes

No

Be sure it is set off with commas. Do not use *that.*

Is the relative pronoun the subject of its own clause?

Yes

No

You should use *who, which,* or *that.* Make the verb agree with the noun to which the relative pronoun refers.

Is the relative pronoun the object of its own clause?

Yes

No

Use *whom, which* or *that,* or omit the pronoun.

(Flowchart continued)

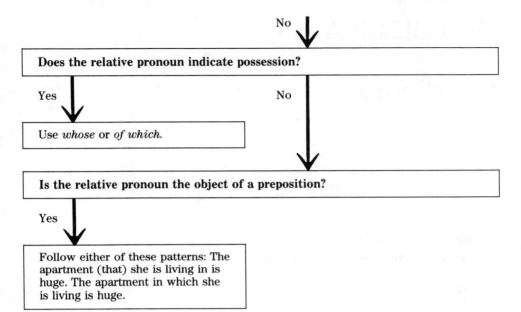

No

Does the relative pronoun indicate possession?

Yes   No

Use *whose* or *of which.*

Is the relative pronoun the object of a preposition?

Yes

Follow either of these patterns: The
apartment (that) she is living in is
huge. The apartment in which she
is living is huge.

TROUBLESPOT 19

Conditions

A. *Types of Conditions*

There are four types of conditions you can express:

fact
future prediction
speculation about present or future
past speculation (contrary to fact)

The type of condition you write depends on the meaning you want to express.

1. The following sentences express conditions of *fact:*

If water freezes, it turns into ice.
If you hear a quick beep, it's the busy signal.
If it's Thursday, I have to go to my exercise class.

2. The following sentences express conditions of *future prediction:*

If the high divorce rate persists, many children will spend some time in a single-parent family.
If I get promoted, I will be very happy.
She might take the job if she can work a shorter day.

3. The following sentences express conditions of *present-future speculation:*

If he gave up his job, he'd have to sell his car.
If I had enough money, I would take a long vacation.
If my grandparents were alive today, they would be shocked by that bathing suit.

When you write sentences like these, the reader should understand them in the following way:

If I had enough money—but I don't—. . .
If my grandparents were alive today—but they aren't—. . .

4. The following sentences express conditions of *past speculation* (contrary to fact):

If she had applied for the management training program last year, she would have learned about financial planning. (But she didn't apply, so she didn't learn about financial planning.)

She wouldn't have paid her employees such high salaries if she had known about financial planning. (But she didn't know about financial planning, so she paid them too much.)

B. Verb Tenses in Conditional Expressions

We can summarize the patterns of conditional verb tenses as shown in the accompanying table. Some other forms can be used, and you will probably come across them in your reading. However, for the purpose of correctness in your own writing, use the table as a guide.

Verbs in Conditional Sentences

Meaning	If clause	Independent clause
Fact	Same tense in both (usually present)	
Future prediction	present	*will* *can* *should* *might* + simple form
Present-future speculation	past *(were)*	*would* *could* etc. + simple form
Past speculation	*had* + participle	*would have* *could have* etc. + participle

Exercise 1

To practice using conditional forms, write a paragraph on each of these topics.

1. If you had $1 million, what would you do?
2. Tell a reader about something you once did that you wish you had not done. How would your life have been different if this had not happened?
3. Think of something that is likely to happen. Tell your reader what will happen as a result if this other event occurs.

Exercise 2

Rewrite the following sentences, using a conditional clause with *if.*

1. I didn't see him, so I didn't pay him the money I owed him. (If I had seen him . . .)
2. She doesn't spend much time with her children, so she doesn't know their friends.
3. They didn't lock the windows; a burglar climbed in and took their jewelry.
4. The woman wasn't able to find an ambulance, so her husband died on the street.
5. He doesn't have anyone to help him, so he won't finish the job on time.

(See Answer Key, p. 166.)

Editing Advice

If you have doubts about the accuracy of the tenses in a sentence with a conditional clause, ask the following questions:

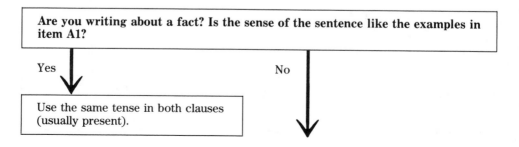

Are you writing about a fact? Is the sense of the sentence like the examples in item A1?

Yes

No

Use the same tense in both clauses (usually present).

(Flowchart continued)

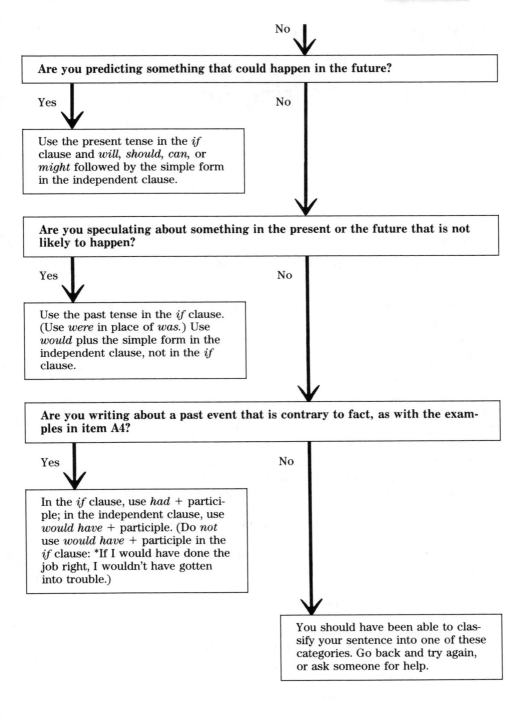

No

Are you predicting something that could happen in the future?

Yes

No

Use the present tense in the *if* clause and *will, should, can,* or *might* followed by the simple form in the independent clause.

Are you speculating about something in the present or the future that is not likely to happen?

Yes

No

Use the past tense in the *if* clause. (Use *were* in place of *was.*) Use *would* plus the simple form in the independent clause, not in the *if* clause.

Are you writing about a past event that is contrary to fact, as with the examples in item A4?

Yes

No

In the *if* clause, use *had* + participle; in the independent clause, use *would have* + participle. (Do *not* use *would have* + participle in the *if* clause: *If I would have done the job right, I wouldn't have gotten into trouble.)

You should have been able to classify your sentence into one of these categories. Go back and try again, or ask someone for help.

TROUBLESPOT 20

Quoting and Citing Sources

Exercise 1

Look at the following passage, from *The Golden Youth of Lee Prince* by Aubrey Goodman.

Mrs. Stein, with her hat on, came back into the room, digging into her purse.

"Marilyn and I are going to that new Italian place," she said, "and I've lost the address. It's that real elegant place where they serve everything burning on a sword."

Priscilla started coughing.

"I think that cough is psychosomatic,°" Lee said.

°**psychosomatic:** caused by a state of mind

Priscilla put a handkerchief to her lips, and Mrs. Stein said, "What does that mean? Does that mean we'll all get it?"

"Probably," Lee said. "Probably."

"Ah, here it is," the woman exclaimed, snatching a piece of paper from her purse. "Priscilla, don't light another cigarette."

Priscilla was moving a hand around in the pocket of her mink coat.

"What's this?" she asked, pulling out a small box. "Lee, it's for you."

She handed him the box, which was from Tiffany's, and he opened it and found a pair of gold cuff links.

Answer the following questions about the passage.

1. How are quotation marks and capital letters used with (a) part of a sentence, (b) a complete sentence, and (c) more than one sentence?
2. What is the relative position of quotation marks and end-of-quotation punctuation?
3. What punctuation separates an introductory phrase like "He said" from a quotation?

4. When is a capital letter used to introduce a quotation—and when isn't one used?
5. With dialogue, when are new paragraphs formed?

(See Answer Key, p. 166.)

A. Direct Quotation

In the passage in Exercise 1, direct quotation is used to record the exact words of a conversation. When you want to record dialogue directly, use direct quotation. You may also want to quote directly when you are writing an essay. Try then to quote directly only passages that are particularly noteworthy or do a great deal to support the point you want to make. You can quote whole sentences or parts of sentences.

Look carefully at the type of material quoted and at the punctuation and capitalization used with the quotation in these examples:

1. That can have important implications for the kids. "In general, the more question-asking the parents do, the higher the children's IQ's," Lewis says. ("The Analysts who Came to Dinner.")
2. Says Atsuko Toyama, author of *A Theory on the Modern Freshman*, "The younger workers do what they are told and not one iota more." (David H. Ahl, "Dulling of the Sword.")
3. In an article about the Japanese work ethic in *Fortune* (May 14, 1984), Lee Smith opines, "In a sense, the rejection of work as a total way of life is not only understandable but healthy." (David H. Ahl, "Dulling of the Sword.")

Check to see if the usage in these examples fits with the answers you gave to the questions in Exercise 1. Note that examples 1 and 2 do not give complete references, with title of work, date of publication, and page numbers; in informal writing and in journalism, that is not always required. Example 3 gives author, source, and date but no page numbers. In academic essays, however, you need to cite the full source for anyone else's ideas that you refer to or quote.

B. Citing Sources and Documentation in Academic Essays

Whenever you quote, you must cite your source. That is, you must tell your reader who said or wrote the words, where they appeared, and when. Sometimes, you might want to refer to an authority but not quote exact words. You might summarize or paraphrase an author's ideas. In the following passage, the author does not quote directly but summarizes an expert's opinion on a controversial issue. However, the author still cites her source and lets us know where she found that opinion expressed.

In fact, based on interviews with hundreds of executives for her book *Paths to Power: A Woman's Guide from First Job to Top Executive* (Addison-Wesley, 1980), Ms. Josefowitz says that women are better managers than men. (Mary Schnack, "Are Women Bosses Better?")

In this passage, the author tells us the title of the book, the author's name, the publisher, and the date of publication. When you write academic essays, you usually give all that information not in the text of your essay but at the end. You need to give your readers all the information they need to locate the source, including the exact page where you found the information.

Various disciplines have guidelines for citing sources and providing documentation. If you have to write a paper for a psychology course, for instance, make sure you ask your instructor what form to use. For essays in the humanities, for instance, the Modern Language Association (MLA) recommends that you give a brief reference in parentheses in your text, so that your reader knows the author's name and the page number. Then, at the end of the essay, you provide a list of works cited (arranged alphabetically by author), giving the full bibliographic details of each source.

The following example is a passage from a student's essay that cites three sources.

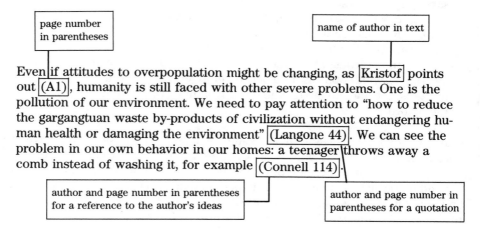

Even if attitudes to overpopulation might be changing, as Kristof points out (A1), humanity is still faced with other severe problems. One is the pollution of our environment. We need to pay attention to "how to reduce the gargantuan waste by-products of civilization without endangering human health or damaging the environment" (Langone 44). We can see the problem in our own behavior in our homes: a teenager throws away a comb instead of washing it, for example (Connell 114).

At the end of the essay, a list of works cited would appear, in alphabetical order. The three entries would look like this:

WORKS CITED

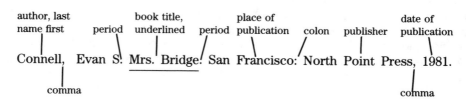

Connell, Evan S. Mrs. Bridge. San Francisco: North Point Press, 1981.

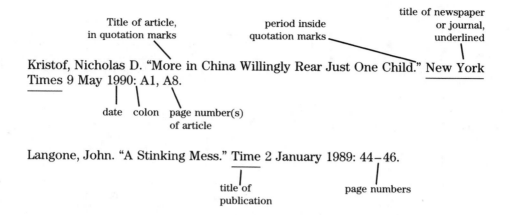

Kristof, Nicholas D. "More in China Willingly Rear Just One Child." New York Times 9 May 1990: A1, A8.

Langone, John. "A Stinking Mess." Time 2 January 1989: 44–46.

title of
publication

page numbers

Exercise 2

Interview somebody about a controversial topic, such as the handling of juvenile criminals, animal rights, or surrogate motherhood. Write an account of the person's views, quoting short, significant comments directly.

Exercise 3

At the library, look up the same controversial topic you used in Exercise 2 in the *Reader's Guide to Periodical Literature*. Find an article that discusses the issue, and write a summary of it, including a few quotations of particularly significant comments. Cite the page number in your summary, and at the end give the exact details of the article in the following order: author, title of article, name of periodical, volume number, date, and page number of the article.

Editing Advice

If you have quoted directly in your piece of writing, ask these questions:

> **Do you think it is better to quote directly than to report the speech? (See also Troublespot 21, "Reporting and Paraphrasing.")**

Yes

No

(Flowchart continued)

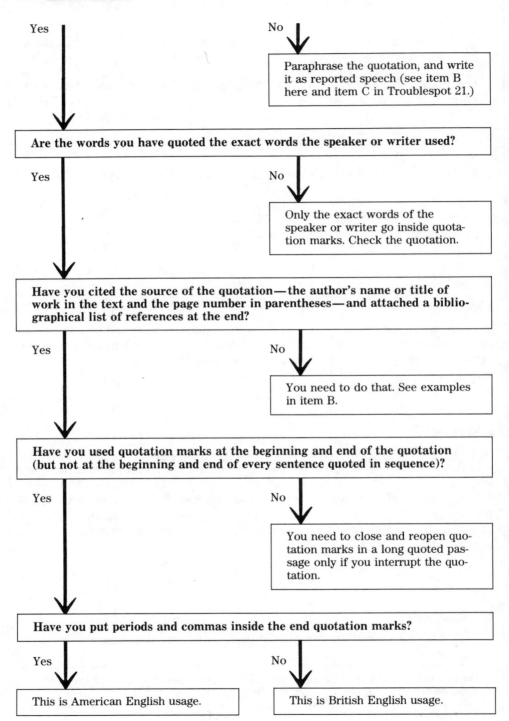

Yes   No

Paraphrase the quotation, and write it as reported speech (see item B here and item C in Troublespot 21.)

Are the words you have quoted the exact words the speaker or writer used?

Yes   No

Only the exact words of the speaker or writer go inside quotation marks. Check the quotation.

Have you cited the source of the quotation—the author's name or title of work in the text and the page number in parentheses—and attached a bibliographical list of references at the end?

Yes   No

You need to do that. See examples in item B.

Have you used quotation marks at the beginning and end of the quotation (but not at the beginning and end of every sentence quoted in sequence)?

Yes   No

You need to close and reopen quotation marks in a long quoted passage only if you interrupt the quotation.

Have you put periods and commas inside the end quotation marks?

Yes   No

This is American English usage.

This is British English usage.

TROUBLESPOT 21

Reporting and Paraphrasing

A. *Direct and Reported Speech*

We use direct quotation when we are writing dialogue or when we are telling the reader exactly what somebody else said or wrote, word for word. We quote exact words when those words are particularly appropriate. If, however, we want to convey general ideas rather than exact words, we usually use reported speech. Note the difference in form:

The mayor asks, "How am I doing?"
The mayor asks how he is doing.

Here the introductory verb is in the present tense. With an introductory verb in the past, we would write this:

The mayor asked how he was doing.

Exercise 1

Look closely at the two sentences below. Count the number of differences you can find between them.

The woman asked, "Where are my glasses?"
The woman asked where her glasses were.

(See Answer Key, p. 167.)

Exercise 2

Look at the cartoon on page 142.
Write a description of each frame of the four-frame cartoon. First, quote di-

© 1959 United Features Syndicate, Inc.

rectly what the characters Lucy and Charlie Brown say, using quotation marks. Begin like this:

> One day Lucy was sitting and offering psychiatric help for 5 cents. Charlie Brown came along, sat down, and said, ". . .

(See Answer Key, p. 167.)

Exercise 3

Now rewrite your description of the cartoon. This time use reported speech. Keep the reported speech as close to the original quotations as possible. Begin like this:

> One day Lucy was sitting and offering psychiatric help for 5 cents. Charlie Brown came along, sat down, and said that . . .

Refer to item B for help.
(See Answer Key, p. 167.)

B. Reported Speech

When you write reported speech, observe the following conventions:

1. Do not use quotation marks.
2. Do not use a question mark at the end of a reported question.
3. In a reported question, use statement word order (subject + verb) and not question word order.
4. After an introductory verb in the past (like *said*), use past tense verbs for the reported speech.
5. Pronouns like *I*, *we*, and *you* change when you write reported speech.
6. *This* and *these* change to *that* and *those*, respectively.
7. Incomplete sentences usually have to be reworded slightly when they are reported.
8. Do not use the same introductory verb every time. Introductory verbs include *say, ask, tell someone to, reply, complain, advise someone to, want to know*, and others.

C. Paraphrase

Usually, when we report speech, we do not simply transform the original words into reported speech. Instead, we tell about the ideas that were expressed, using our own words. That is, we paraphrase. A paraphrased report might look like this:

One day, when Lucy was offering psychiatric help for 5 cents, Charlie Brown visited her booth and complained of depression. He wanted advice on how to deal with it, but Lucy simply urged him not to be depressed— and charged him 5 cents anyway!

D. Cite Sources to Avoid Plagiarism

In an essay, always state where ideas come from. Even if you do not quote another writer word for word but instead refer to and paraphrase his or her ideas, you still have to say where those ideas came from. You must state the name of the author, the title of the work, the place and date of publication, and the publisher. You do this by mentioning the author or title and the page number in parentheses in your text and then giving the full bibliographic reference at the end of the paper. (See item B in Troublespot 20 for examples.) Using another author's words or ideas as your own and not citing the source is *plagiarism*. This is *not acceptable* and probably illegal. For different methods of citing the sources of your ideas, consult your instructor or a handbook.

Exercise 4

Look at the passage from *The Golden Youth of Lee Prince* on p. 136. With the book open in front of you, rewrite the passage, changing all the direct speech to reported speech. Use no direct quotations at all. Begin like this:

> Mrs. Stein told the people in the room that she and Marilyn were going to a new Italian restaurant . . .

(See Answer Key, p. 167.)

Exercise 5

Now close the book and write another account of the conversation you rewrote in Exercise 4. This time, rely on your memory. Paraphrase the passage, and do not use any direct quotations. Concentrate on conveying the main gist of the conversation. The reporting does not have to be an exact sentence-by-sentence replica of the original.

Editing Advice

If you have written about what somebody else said or wrote, ask these questions:

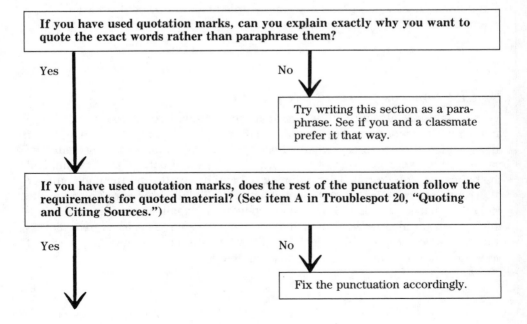

```
┌──────────────────────────────────────────────────────────────┐
│ If you have used quotation marks, can you explain exactly     │
│ why you want to quote the exact words rather than paraphrase  │
│ them?                                                          │
└──────────────────────────────────────────────────────────────┘
     Yes                          No
      │                            │
      │                            ▼
      │              ┌────────────────────────────────┐
      │              │ Try writing this section as a   │
      │              │ paraphrase. See if you and a    │
      │              │ classmate prefer it that way.   │
      │              └────────────────────────────────┘
      ▼
┌──────────────────────────────────────────────────────────────┐
│ If you have used quotation marks, does the rest of the        │
│ punctuation follow the requirements for quoted material?      │
│ (See item A in Troublespot 20, "Quoting and Citing Sources.") │
└──────────────────────────────────────────────────────────────┘
     Yes                          No
      │                            │
      │                            ▼
      │              ┌────────────────────────────────┐
      │              │ Fix the punctuation             │
      │              │ accordingly.                    │
      │              └────────────────────────────────┘
      ▼
```

(Flowchart continued)

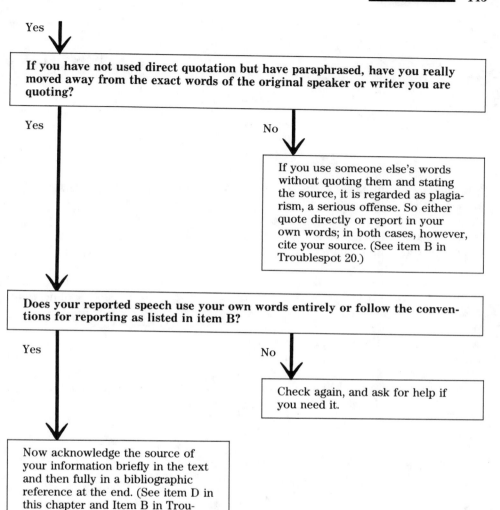

Yes

If you have not used direct quotation but have paraphrased, have you really moved away from the exact words of the original speaker or writer you are quoting?

Yes

No

If you use someone else's words without quoting them and stating the source, it is regarded as plagiarism, a serious offense. So either quote directly or report in your own words; in both cases, however, cite your source. (See item B in Troublespot 20.)

Does your reported speech use your own words entirely or follow the conventions for reporting as listed in item B?

Yes

No

Check again, and ask for help if you need it.

Now acknowledge the source of your information briefly in the text and then fully in a bibliographic reference at the end. (See item D in this chapter and Item B in Troublespot 20.)

Works Cited

Ahl, David, H. "Dulling of the Sword." *Creative Computing*, 1984, p. 467.

"The Analysts Who Came to Dinner." *Newsweek*, October 19, 1981, p. 92.

Baker, Russell. *Growing Up*. Congdon & Weed, Chicago, 1982, p. 42–43.

Beer, William. *Househusbands*. J. F. Bergin Publishers, 1983, pp. xix–xx.

Connell, Evan S. *Mrs. Bridge*, San Francisco: North Point Press, 1959, pp. 14–16, 113–114.

Doherty, Jim. "Mr. Doherty Builds His Dream Life." *Money*, May 1982, pp. 77.

Goodman, Aubrey. *The Golden Youth of Lee Prince*. Greenwich, Connecticut: Crest Books, 1959, p. 312.

Mencken, H.L. *Smart Set Criticism*. Cornell University Press, 1968.

Schnack, Mary. "Are Women Bosses Better?" *McCall's*, 1981, p. 39.

Sidel, Ruth. *Women and Children Last: The Plight of Poor Women in Affluent America*. Viking Penguin, 1986, 5–7, 61–62.

Sorrentino, Constance. "Changing Family in International Perspective," *Monthly Labor Review*, March 1990, pp. 41–44.

Zongren, Liu. *Two Years in the Melting Pot*. China Books, 1984, pp. 26–29.

Appendix

APPENDIX

Irregular Verbs

The -*s* and -*ing* forms of irregular verbs have been included only in instances where the spelling sometimes causes students trouble.

Simple Form	-s	-ing	Past	Participle
arise		arising	arose	arisen
be		being	was,were	been
beat		beating	beat	beaten
become		becoming	became	become
begin		beginning	began	begun
bend			bent	bent
bet		betting	bet	bet
bind			bound	bound
bite		biting	bit	bitten
bleed			bled	bled
blow			blew	blown
break			broke	broken
breed			bred	bred
bring			brought	brought
build			built	built
burst			burst	burst
buy			bought	bought
catch			caught	caught
choose		choosing	chose	chosen
cling			clung	clung
come		coming	came	come
cost	costs		cost	cost
creep		creeping	crept	crept
cut		cutting	cut	cut
deal			dealt	dealt
dig		digging	dug	dug
do	does		did	done
draw			drew	drawn
drink			drank	drunk
drive		driving	drove	driven

Simple Form	-s	-ing	Past	Participle
eat		eating	ate	eaten
fall			fell	fallen
feed			fed	fed
feel		feeling	felt	felt
fight			fought	fought
find			found	found
flee			fled	fled
fly	flies	flying	flew	flown
forbid		forbidding	forbad(e)	forbidden
forget		forgetting	forgot	forgotten
forgive		forgiving	forgave	forgiven
freeze		freezing	froze	frozen
get		getting	got	gotten, got
give		giving	gave	given
go			went	gone
grind			ground	ground
grow			grew	grown
hang*			hung	hung
have		having	had	had
hear			heard	heard
hide		hiding	hid	hidden
hit		hitting	hit	hit
hold			held	held
hurt			hurt	hurt
keep			kept	kept
know			knew	known
lay		laying	laid	laid
lead			led	led
leave		leaving	left	left
lend			lent	lent
let		letting	let	let
lie		lying	lay	lain
light			lit, lighted	lit, lighted
lose		losing	lost	lost
make		making	made	made
mean			meant	meant
meet		meeting	met	met
pay	pays		paid	paid
put		putting	put	put
quit		quitting	quit	quit
read		reading	read	read
ride		riding	rode	ridden
ring			rang	rung
rise		rising	rose	risen
run		running	ran	run
say	says		said	said

*Hang in the sense "put to death" is regular: hang, hanged, hanged.

Simple Form	-s	-ing	Past	Participle
see			saw	seen
seek			sought	sought
sell			sold	sold
send			sent	sent
set		setting	set	set
shake		shaking	shook	shaken
shine		shining	shone	shone
shoot			shot	shot
show			showed	shown, showed
shrink			shrank	shrunk
shut		shutting	shut	shut
sing			sang	sung
sink			sank	sunk
sit		sitting	sat	sat
sleep		sleeping	slept	slept
slide		sliding	slid	slid
slit		slitting	slit	slit
speak			spoke	spoken
spend			spent	spent
spin		spinning	spun	spun
spit		spitting	spit	spit
split		splitting	split	split
spread			spread	spread
spring			sprang	sprung
stand			stood	stood
steal		stealing	stole	stolen
stick			stuck	stuck
sting			stung	stung
stink			stank	stunk
strike		striking	struck	struck
swear			swore	sworn
sweep		sweeping	swept	swept
swim		swimming	swam	swum
swing			swung	swung
take		taking	took	taken
teach			taught	taught
tear			tore	torn
tell			told	told
think			thought	thought
throw			threw	thrown
tread			trod	trodden, trod
understand			understood	understood
upset		upsetting	upset	upset
wake		waking	woke	waked, woken
wear			wore	worn
weave		weaving	wove	woven

Simple Form	-s	-ing	Past	Participle
weep		weeping	wept	wept
win		winning	won	won
wind			wound	wound
withdraw			withdrew	withdrawn
wring			wrung	wrung
write		writing	wrote	written

Answer Key

Note: There is often more than one correct answer to an exercise. If your answer is different from the answer here, do not assume that your answer is wrong. You may have found an alternative solution. Check with your instructor.

Troublespot 1: Basic Sentence Structure

Exercise 1: Identify Standard Sentences in Written English

Note: There are more possibilities than those given here. If you have other versions, check them with your instructor.

1. The sun is shining.
2. They walk slowly and quietly.
3. They watch themselves make steps on the white sand. (OR They walk slowly and quietly, watching themselves make steps on the white sand.)
4. OK
5. You can hardly see any sand because there are so many people and so many umbrellas.
6. OK
7. You can imagine walking on the white glittering sand with the feeling of (OR sand, feeling) cool sand running through your toes.
8. OK
9. There are some leaves on the sand.
10. It is a St. Croix beach in the Virgin Islands.
11. The tree on the beach is very big.
12. Some umbrellas provide shade from the sun.
13. On that beach, two people are enjoying the beautiful weather.
14. The sun is shining.
15. OK

Exercise 2: Divide Sentences into Subject and Predicate

1. We / lived in Shin-Ying.
2. The front door of the house   /   faced the front gate . . .
3. My mother   /   taught at the school.
4. Cleaning up the fallen leaves   /   was my job.
5. My family   /   sat around under the grapevine.

Exercise 3: Find and Correct Fragments

1. (b) is a fragment. Because there are many trees, the dark scenery could frighten us.
2. (b) is a fragment. He is working at the gas pumps to try to fix what is wrong.
3. (b) is a fragment. Replace the period at the end of (a) with a comma, and lowercase *one.*
4. OK
5. (a) is a fragment. On that beach, two young people are strolling . . .

Exercise 5: Identify Standard Sentences and Correct Errors

1. OK
2. (b) is a fragment. Omit the period at the end of (a) and lowercase *because.*
3. Fragment. They are eating very slowly.
4. Repeated subject. The children who were eating the ice cream were with my uncle.
5. No subject. Usually in the summer it is very hot in the city.
6. Word order. Every week she spends a lot of money. OR She spends a lot of money every week.
7. Word order. He likes his sister's friend very much.
8. Word order with indirect objects. She gave her sister an expensive present. OR She gave an expensive present to her sister.
9. Parallel structures. . . . without noise, pollution, crowds, dirt, and humidity.
10. Fragment: no complete verb. The smell of frying hot dogs fills (filled) my nostrils and makes (made) me hungry.

Troublespot 2: Connecting Sentences with Coordinating Conjunctions and Transitions

Exercise 1: List Transitions and Purpose

1. indeed: emphasizes
2. however: points out a contrast
3. in fact: emphasizes by giving a specific example
4. for example: provides an example
5. consequently: shows result

Exercise 2: Connect Sentences

Several solutions for each pair are possible; only one is given here.
1. . . . writer; for instance, he always wrote standing up.
2. . . . writer; in addition, he was an active sportsman.
3. . . . paper. However, he shifted to his typewriter . . .
4. . . . glance. He was, nevertheless, a neat person at heart.
5. . . . him; in fact, he hardly ever threw anything away.
6. . . . novels; for example, he rewrote the ending of *A Farewell to Arms* 39 times.
7. . . . morning. Then, after lunch, . . .
8. . . . stopping. As a result, his landlady worried that he wasn't eating enough.

Exercise 3: Connect or Combine Sentences

Several solutions for each type of combination are possible; only one is given here.
1. He injured his knee, but he decided . . .
   He injured his knee; however, he decided . . .
2. They visited France, Italy, and Spain, and they managed . . .
   They visited France, Italy, and Spain; they also managed . . .
3. Their money was stolen, but they got it all back because . . .
   Their money was stolen. They got it all back, though, because . . .
4. She wanted to pass her exams, so she studied . . .
   She wanted to pass her exams; consequently, she studied . . .
5. She studied very hard, but she didn't pass her examinations.
   She studied very hard; however, she didn't pass her examinations.

Exercise 4: Identify Correct Sentences

1. CS
2. RO
3. CS
4. OK
5. CS

Troublespot 3: Combining Sentences with Subordinating Conjunctions

Exercise 1: Connect or Combine Sentences

Some of the possibilities are listed here.
1. . . . students, but what . . .
   . . . students. However, . . .
   . . . students. What they really need, however, is . . .
   Although teachers say they want diligent students, what they . . .
2. . . . late, so my boss . . .
   Whenever I arrive late, my boss . . .
   . . . late; as a result, my boss . . .
   . . . late. Consequently, my boss . . .
3. . . . money, so he bought . . .
   As soon as he won some money, he bought . . .
   Because he had won some money, he bought . . .
   . . . money. Therefore, he bought . . .
4. . . . sick, but I didn't.
   Although everyone in my family got sick, I didn't.
   . . . sick; however, I didn't.
   . . . sick; I, however, didn't.
5. . . . prize, but she was proud of her work.
   . . . prize. Nevertheless, she was proud of her work.
   Even though my sister didn't win the essay prize, she was proud of her work.
6. Prices went up, and demand went down.
   Prices went up, so demand went down.
   When prices went up, demand went down.

As soon as prices went up, demand went down.
Prices went up; then demand went down.
7. . . . paycheck, and she left . . .
    . . . paycheck, so she left . . .
   When she got her paycheck, she left . . .
    . . . paycheck; then she left . . .
8. . . . robbery, so they were . . .
    . . . robbery; as a result, they were . . .
   Since they were found guilty of robbery, they were . . .
9. . . . dealings, but he was not . . .
    . . . dealings; however, he was not . . .
   Although he made a lot . . ., he was not . . .
10. . . . resources, so there was . . .
   He wasted so many of the company's resources that there was . . .
    . . . resources. As a result, there was . . .

Exercise 2: Combine Sentences

Here are a few of the possibilities.
To make a good impression, Jack, the new head clerk, wore his brother's new suit, but
   the pants kept falling down because the suit was too big for him.
Since Jack, the new head clerk, wanted to make a good impression, he wore his brother's new suit; however, the pants kept falling down because the suit was too big
   for him.
Although the new head clerk, Jack, wore a new suit belonging to his brother in order to
   make a good impression, the suit was too big for him, so the pants kept falling
   down.

Exercise 3: Examine Sentence Structure

1. There are two independent clauses: Jack wore his brother's new suit. / The suit was
   so big for him.
2. *Jack wore* and *the suit was*
3. The independent clauses are connected by *but.*
4. There is one subordinate clause: *that the pants kept falling down* (result).
5. Other attachments are condensed phrases: *intending to make a good impression* and
   the new head clerk.

Exercise 4: Combine Sentences

Only one or two possibilities for each group of sentences is given here. There are
others. Check with your instructor to find out if your versions are accurate.
1. As I watched a little girl carrying a big shopping bag, I felt so sorry for her that I offered to help.
2. When my huge family met at my grandparents' house every holiday, there were never
   enough chairs, so I always had to sit on the floor.
3. Computers save so much time that many businesses are buying them, but the managers sometimes don't realize that they have to train people to operate the machines.

4. All their lives they have lived with their father, a powerful politician who has made lots of enemies.

5. Wanting to be successful, she worked day and night for a famous advertising agency until eventually she became a vice-president.

6. Although he really wants to go skiing, he has decided to go to a beach resort in California since his sister, whom he hasn't seen for ten years, lives there. OR Although he really wants to go skiing, he has decided to go to a beach resort in California to visit his sister, whom he hasn't seen for ten years.

Troublespot 4: Punctuation

Exercise 1: Fit Commas into Categories

1. The comma sets off a phrase before the subject of the sentence.
2. The comma sets off inserted material.
3. The comma separates independent clauses.
4. The comma separates items in a list.
5. The comma sets off a phrase and a clause before the subject of the sentence.
6. The comma sets off a phrase before the subject.
7. The comma separates items in a list.
8. The comma sets off a phrase before the subject.
9–13. The commas set off inserted material.

Exercise 2: Rewrite with Apostrophes

1. the baby's toys
2. the babies' toys
3. the teachers' problems
4. my family's decision
5. the women's plans
6. the politicians' proposals
7. the secretary's desk
8. the couple's home
9. the people's park
10. the little boy's ball

Exercise 3: Add Punctuation Marks

The study also offers a clue to why middle children often seem to have a harder time in life than their siblings. Lewis found that in families with three or four children, dinner conversation tends to center on the oldest child, who has the most to talk about, and the youngest, who needs the most attention. "Middle children are invisible," says Lewis. "When you see someone get up from the table and walk around during dinner, chances are it's the middle child." There is, however, one great equalizer that stops all conversation and deprives everyone of attention: "When the TV is on," Lewis says, "dinner is a non-event."

Despite the feminist movement, Lewis's study indicates that preparing dinner continues to be regarded as woman's work—even when both spouses have jobs. Some men do help out, but for most husbands dinnertime remains a relaxing hour.

Troublespot 5: Verb Tenses: Tense and Time

Exercise 1: Identify the Context for a Switch in Time

The writer signaled the switch in time with the word *once*, telling us that she was going to describe an event in the past.

Exercise 2: Identify Verb Phrase, Time Cluster, Time Relationship, and Signal

love: present, simple tense
watch: present, simple tense
can get: present, simple tense
was: past, simple tense (signal: three months ago)
spent: past, simple tense (modal)
will be: future, simple tense (signal: three months from now)
will be cultivating, weeding, killing: future, in progress at a known time in the future
had to reshingle: past, simple tense (signal: recently)
will help: future, simple tense (signal: soon)
supplements: present, simple tense
are working: present, in progress at a known time in the present and future
will spray, paint, plant, clean: future, simple tense (signal: later this month)
arrive: future, simple present tense (in time clause)

Troublespot 6: Verb Tenses: Present-Future

Exercise 1: Select Correct Verb Tense

1. play
2. understands
3. ends
4. goes
5. needs
6. is wearing
7. looks
8. begins
9. make
10. are making

Exercise 2: Supply the Present Perfect

1. have served
2. have grown
3. (have) shaved
4. have eaten
5. have made
6. have written
7. have written
8. (have) published
9. (have) reviewed
10. have had

Exercise 3: Correct the Errors

1. has been working
2. wear
3. cause
4. teach
5. is sitting
6. are trying
7. has been
8. have been sitting
9. get
10. do

Troublespot 7: Agreement

Exercise 1: Identify Verbs and Change the Subjects

The verbs are *pursues, oversees, bakes, cans, freezes, chauffeurs, practices, takes, does, writes, tends, stacks,* and *delivers.*

With a plural subject *(Sandy and her sister)*, all these verbs will change to the no -*s* form: *pursue, oversee,* etc. Other changes: *her* becomes *their, she* becomes *they, herself* becomes *themselves.*

Exercise 2: Select *There Is* or *There Are*

1. are		6. is	
2. is		7. are	
3. is		8. are	
4. is		9. is	
5. are		10. are	

Exercise 3: Select Correct Verb Form

1. comes	6. costs
2. want	7. have
3. has	8. tries
4. requires	9. was
5. know	10. wants, is

Troublespot 8: Verb Tenses: Past

Exercises 1 and 2: Rewrite the Passage in the Past and Identify the Time of Each Verb

The following changes need to be made:
have: had, simple past
are taking: were taking, past progressive
work: were working, progressive OR worked, simple past
will be: would be, modal past
arrive: arrived, simple past
want: wanted, simple past
is: was, simple past
have to do: had to do, modal past
have come: had come, past perfect
are trying: were trying, past progressive
are: were, simple past
think: thought, simple past
will succeed: would succeed, modal past

Exercise 4: Insert Past Verb Forms

1. was	7. enjoyed	13. slipped
2. took (would take)	8. learned	14. disappeared
3. spent (would spend)	9. were playing	15. said
4. played	10. fell	16. would never forget
5. grew	11. had	17. did
6. did not know	12. was trying	

Troublespot 9: Active and Passive

Exercise 1: Identify Complete Verbs and Classify as Active or Passive

1. take: active
   can be slowed: passive
   are cut: passive
   will increase: active
   is banned: passive
   is enforced: passive
   will be tainted: passive
   have been released: passive
2. were taught: passive
   resisted: active
   made sure: active

Exercise 2: Rewrite Sentences Using the Passive

1. A lot of changes have been made in the curriculum.
2. Some popular courses have been canceled.
3. A lot of rice is grown in Japan.
4. The suspect is being questioned right now.
5. The budget will be revised within the next few months.

Troublespot 10: Modal Auxiliaries

Exercise 4: Identify the Difference in Meaning

1. (a) It is prohibited. (The computer might give you an electric shock.)
   (b) You are allowed to, but it is not necessary. You can use a typewriter instead.
2. (a) It is advisable, but it is your choice.
   (b) It is necessary. (You will not get your passport without it.)
3. (a) His results are questionable. It is possible that someone will challenge them.
   (b) His results do not seem possible, and his research methods were very sloppy. Someone has to challenge them. (It is necessary or logical that this will happen.)
   (c) His results come from such a badly designed experiment that anyone would be advised to challenge them.
   (d) He did this experiment in the past. He did not do it well. But surprisingly, nobody challenged his results.
4. (a) But she didn't, so now she can't go with us on vacation.
   (b) I don't know if she did or not. It is possible.
   (c) She never seems to spend anything, so I assume that she has saved her money.
   (d) She has very rich parents. They paid for her vacation.
   (e) She was in debt and had bills to pay. The only way she could pay was to save most of her salary each month.
5. (a) It was necessary; her teacher referred her and set up an appointment.
   (b) It seems strongly advisable. Her teacher will tell her that it is a good idea.
   (c) It was not necessary for her to see a psychiatrist; a therapist was able to help her.

Troublespot 11: Verb Forms

Exercise 1: Identify Complete Verb

1. is said, experienced, appeared, were planning, had invited, would begin
2. have entered, are thought, were isolated, replicate, are, have been thought, has encouraged

Exercise 2: Complete the Sentences

1. intend
2. pay
3. been
4. are
5. being

Exercise 3: Complete the Sentences

1. lying
2. raised
3. fell
4. did
5. doesn't

Troublespot 12: Nouns and Quantity Words

Exercise 1: Identify and Categorize Nouns

1. *luxuries:* C, count, pl
   boyhood: C, count, s
   women: C, count, pl
   life: C, unc
   rewards: C, count, pl
2. *mother:* C, count, s
   grandmother: C, count, s
   house: C, unc (idiom = to keep house)
   women: C, count, pl
   Civil War: P
3. *electricity:* C, unc
   gas: C, unc
   plumbing: C, unc
   heating: C, unc
4. *baths:* C, count, pl
   laundry: C, unc
   dishwashing: C, unc
   buckets: C, count, pl
   water: C, unc
   spring: C, count, s
   foot: C, count, s
   hill: C, count, s

5. *floors:* C, count, pl
  hands: C, count, pl
  knees: C, count, pl
  rugs: C, count, pl
  carpet beaters: C, count, pl
  chickens: C, count, pl
  bread: C, unc
  pastries: C, count, pl
  clothing: C, unc
  treadle: C, count, s (used here as part of a compound adjective)
  sewing machines: C, count, pl
6. *end:* C, count, s
  day: C, count, s
  woman: C, count, s
  serf: C, count, s
7. *[men]:* C, count, pl
  basins: C, count, pl
  supper: C, unc
  porch: C, count, s
  night: C, count, s
8. *women:* C, count, pl
  twilight: C, unc (used here as an adjective)
  music: C, unc
  Morrisonville: P

Exercise 2: Identify Mistakes with Noun Capitals and Plurals

Correction of errors:
suitcase: suitcases
store: stores
Town: town
dress: dresses
spain: Spain

Troublespot 13: Articles

Exercise 1: Categorize Articles and Determiners with Nouns

families: countable, plural, nonspecific
their members: countable, plural, possessive adjective, specific
a lot of support: uncountable, quantity word, nonspecific
a child: countable, singular, nonspecific
a fight: countable, singular, nonspecific
a friend: countable, singular, nonspecific
his mother: countable, singular, possessive adjective, specific
home: idiom: at home
an aunt: countable, singular, nonspecific
a grandmother: countable, singular, nonspecific
advice: uncountable, nonspecific

six years: countable, plural, numeral, specific
my bicycle: countable, singular, possessive adjective, specific
the block: countable, singular, specific
a race: countable, singular, nonspecific
my friends: countable, plural, possessive adjective, specific
my father: countable, singular, possessive adjective, specific
my mother: countable, singular, possessive adjective, specific
the house: countable, singular, specific
people: countable (one person, two people), plural, nonspecific
my aunt: countable, singular, possessive adjective, specific
my knees: countable, plural, possessive adjective, specific
my grandmother: countable, singular, possessive adjective, specific
a glass: countable, singular, nonspecific
milk: uncountable, nonspecific
a cookie: countable, singular, nonspecific
my uncle: countable, singular, possessive adjective, specific
the doctor's office: countable, singular, possessive noun, specific

Exercise 3: Insert Articles

1. a. a
   b. —
   c. The
   d. the
   e. the
2. a. a
   b. the
   c. the
   d. —
   e. a
   f. a
   g. the
   h. —
   i. —

Troublespot 14: Pronouns and Reference

Exercise 1: Answer Questions

1. the one just described, with the run-over heels, etc.
2. the fact that women held so few management positions

Exercise 2: Identify Pronouns and Adjectives and Their Referents

1. they: parents
   their: parents
   them: children
2. this: pollution
   they: many people

3. He: a new manager
   him: a new manager
4. his: the father
   their: the father and his son
5. their: children
   They: children
   they: children
   them: children

Troublespot 15: Adjectives and Adverbs

Exercise 1: Determine Categories of Adjectives in Noun Phrases

1. that: determiner
   sophisticated: opinion
   young: age
   Italian: nationality
   model: head noun
2. his: determiner
   comfortable: opinion
   white: color
   velvet: material
   couch: head noun
3. two: determiner
   middle-aged: age
   Catholic: religion
   bishops: head noun
4. their: determiner
   charming: opinion
   little: size
   wood: material
   cabin: head noun

Troublespot 16: Infinitive, -ing, and Participle Forms

Exercise 1: Insert Correct Verb Form

1. to arrange
2. to wait
3. having
4. writing
5. being
6. to lie
7. close
8. to prevent
9. to make
10. skating

Exercise 2: Write Sentences

Possible answers:
1. The loud radio annoyed Sarah.
   Sarah found the loud radio annoying.
   Sarah was annoyed by the loud radio.
2. The difficult lecture confused the students.
   The difficult lecture was confusing for the students.
   The students were confused by the difficult lecture.
3. The end of the movie surprised us.
   We thought the end of the movie was surprising.
   We were surprised by the end of the movie.

Exercise 3: Insert Correct Form

1. a. collecting
   b. fishing
   c. enjoying
   d. found
   e. looking
2. a. adjusting
   b. doing
   c. been
   d. obliged
   e. to do
   f. having
   g. to play
   h. taking
3. a. adjusting
   b. dealing
   c. relying
   d. waiting
   e. caused
   f. allowed
   g. to progress
   h. to be

Exercise 4: Combine Sentences

1. Wanting to get the job, she arrived early for the interview.
2. The gray-haired woman wearing a blue coat is my mother.
3. We saw an exciting movie last week.
4. Confused by the examination questions, the student failed the exam.
5. The painting stolen from the museum yesterday was extremely valuable.

Troublespot 17: Prepositions and Phrasal Verbs

Exercise 1: Insert a Preposition

1. in
2. on
3. at
4. off
5. during
6. at
7. of
8. on
9. in
10. of

Exercise 3: Insert a Word

1. off
2. by
3. seeing
4. up, off
5. after
6. on winning
7. it on
8. to, until, in
9. on, for asking
10. to, about

Troublespot 18: Relative Clauses

Exercise 1: Combine Sentences with a Relative Clause

Only one method of combining is given here. Others are possible. Check with your instructor.

1. The man who won the race was awarded a prize.
2. The girl who is sitting in the front row asks a lot of questions.
3. The people (that) I met at a party last night are from California.
4. The house (that) he is living in is gigantic.
5. Mrs. McHam, who lives next door to me, is a lawyer.
6. The journalist whose story you read yesterday has won a lot of prizes.
7. The radio (that) I bought was made in Taiwan.
8. She told her friends about the book (that) she had just read.
9. The man whose dog I am looking after is a radio announcer.
10. The pediatrician (that/whom) I recommended lives in my neighborhood.

Exercise 2: Correct the Errors

1. Two years ago, my friend Zhi-Wei, who had just gotten married, worked as a manager in a big company.

2. A boy from high school who was the worst person in the class took another boy's sweater.
3. My sister, who's living in Atlanta, writes to me every week.
4. I have found the book that I was looking for.
5. The students in my class who study hard will pass the test.

Exercise 3: Combine Sentences with a Relative Clause

1. Thirty-three people, most of whom lived in the neighborhood, attended the lecture.
2. They waited half an hour for the committee members, some of whom just did not show up.
3. I sang three songs, one of which was "Singing in the Rain."
4. The statewide poetry competition was held last month, and she submitted four poems, none of which won a prize.
5. On every wall of his house he has hundreds of books, most of which are detective novels.

Troublespot 19: Conditions

Exercise 2: Rewrite with a Conditional Clause

1. If I had seen him, I would have paid him the money I owed him.
2. If she spent more time with her children, she would know their friends.
3. If they had locked the windows, a burglar would not have climbed in and taken their jewelry.
4. If the woman had been able to find an ambulance, her husband wouldn't have died on the street.
5. If he had someone to help him, he would finish the job on time.

Troublespot 20: Quoting and Citing Sources

Exercise 1: Answer Questions

1. (a) When part of a sentence is quoted, the part does not begin with a capital letter: "and I've lost the address. . . ."
   (b) When a whole sentence is quoted, it begins with a capital letter, it begins and ends with quotation marks, and the quotation marks come after the punctuation that signals the end of the quotation: "What's this?" she asked. A quoted complete sentence that does not appear at the end of the written sentence ends in a comma, not a period: "Ah, here it is," the woman exclaimed.
   (c) When more than one sentence is quoted, quotation marks do not appear at the beginning and end of every sentence but only at the beginning and end of the passage quoted: Mrs. Stein said, "What does that mean? Does that mean we'll all get it?"
2. Quotation marks regularly come after the end-of-quotation punctuation: "Marilyn and I are going to that new Italian place," she said.
3. A comma: Mrs. Stein said, "What does that mean? . . ."
4. A capital letter is used when a complete sentence is quoted. If the quotation begins in the middle of a sentence, no capital letter is used: "Marilyn and I are going to that new Italian place," she said, "and I've lost the address. . . ."
5. A new paragraph marks a change of speaker.

Troublespot 21: Reporting and Paraphrasing

Exercise 1: Determine the Differences in the Sentences

There are seven differences in the second sentence: no comma, no capital letter for *where*, no quotation marks, *are/were*, *my/her*, statement word order, no question mark.

Exercise 2: Quote Directly

One version:

Charlie Brown came along, sat down, and said, "I have deep feelings of depression." Then he asked, "What can I do about this?" Lucy replied, "Snap out of it! Five cents, please."

Exercise 3: Change to Reported Speech

One version, providing an example of a reported statement, question, and command:

Charlie Brown came along, sat down, and said that he had deep feelings of depression. He asked Lucy what he could do about that. She advised him to snap out of it and politely asked him for five cents.

Exercise 4: Change to Reported Speech

One version follows. Others are possible.

Mrs. Stein told the people in the room that she and Marilyn were going to a new Italian restaurant, an elegant place where they served everything burning on a sword. However, she had lost the address. At that point, Priscilla started coughing, and Lee wondered aloud if the cough was psychosomatic. Mrs. Stein didn't know what that word meant and wanted to know if they would all get the cough. Lee said they probably would. Suddenly, Mrs. Stein found the piece of paper with the address on it. As Priscilla put her hand in her mink-coat pocket, Mrs. Stein told her not to light another cigarette, but Priscilla pulled out a little box and told Lee it was for him. It was a Tiffany's box, and in it he found a pair of gold cuff links.

Index